*An Indictment, Alternate Budget Proposal,
and Citizen's Guide to Action*

RONALD REAGAN
AND THE
AMERICAN ENVIRONMENT

An Indictment prepared by

*Friends of the Earth • Natural Resources Defense Council
The Wilderness Society • Sierra Club
National Audubon Society • Environmental Defense Fund
Environmental Policy Center • Environmental Action
Defenders of Wildlife • Solar Lobby*

FRIENDS OF THE EARTH ⊕ SAN FRANCISCO

Published by Brick House Publishing Company

Copyright © 1982 by *Friends of the Earth*

Trade Sales and Distribution by
Brick House Publishing Co., Inc.
34 Essex Street
Andover, MA 01810

Library of Congress Cataloging in Publication Data:

Main entry under title:

Ronald Reagan and the American environment.

   Includes bibliographical references.

   1. Environmental policy—United States 2. United
States—Economic policy—1981–   . I. Friends of the
Earth.
HC110.E5R659 1982   363.7'056'0973   82-20723
ISBN 0–931790–43–3

CONTENTS

Indictment   5

The Reagan Energy Plan:
A Major Power Failure   37
   References   79

Alternative Budget Proposals   85

Citizens Guide to Action   139

About Friends of the Earth   144

Indictment

The Case Against the Reagan Environmental Record

Friends of the Earth
Natural Resources Defense Council
The Wilderness Society
Sierra Club
National Audubon Society
Environmental Defense Fund
Environmental Policy Center
Environmental Action
Defenders of Wildlife
Solar Lobby

March 1982

Introduction

President Reagan has broken faith with the American people on environmental protection. During his first 14 months in office, he and his appointed officials have simply refused to do the job that the laws require and that Americans expect of their government—to protect the public health from pollution and to use publicly owned resources and lands for the public good. Instead, Reagan Administration officials are handing over to private use the clean air and water, forests, grasslands, coal and oil that belong to us all. In the name of "getting the government off our backs," they are giving away our natural heritage.

We have watched for a year as the Administration took or proposed scores of actions that veered radically away from the broad bipartisan consensus in support of environmental protection that has existed for many years. We thought it time to examine the entire record. We began with apprehension. We end appalled.

The pages that follow document hundreds of actions that endanger the quality of life of all Americans. These separate actions add up to the Reagan environmental record. It is difficult to read that record without sorrow, anger, and a real concern for our future.

Pollution will increase because the rules designed to control it and the agencies that enforce the rules are being systematically weakened. The Administration's attention has focused upon easing the burdens for polluters instead of protecting the public and the land.

The Administration has moved swiftly. It has changed clean air rules to allow many coal-burning plants to dump more sulfur dioxide into the air, where it re-forms as acid rain. It has withdrawn rules to control industries that dump toxic chemical wastes into landfills or flush them into city wastewater plants where they corrode equipment. From strip mines to waste dumps the Administration has cut back enforcement of the laws. Its agencies make fewer inspections and take many fewer illegal polluters to court.

When it could not get Congress to change the environmental laws, the Administration used budget cuts to cripple the agencies that carry them out. Eight major statutes passed in the last 12 years assign to EPA a job that will double in size in the next few years. The Administration wants to slash EPA's budget by 40 percent. The job will not get done and the cost in terms of sickness, death and material destruction will be very great.

A century ago, the federal government was giving away public lands and their resources practically free of charge. Since then, the American people have come to see their public lands as a priceless resource to be used for the long-term benefit of all. A succession of laws over many decades has directed that these lands be used for wilderness, wildlife habitat, recreation, watershed protection and scenic beauty, as well as for minerals production, timber cutting, and livestock grazing. The law requires management of public forestland and grasslands to protect the long-term interests of the public and assure that private use does not destroy the land's long-term productivity.

The Reagan Administration has made a mockery of the multiple-use/sustained-yield concept that governs the public lands. It has put huge amounts of the nation's coal, oil and timber up for sale at bargain basement prices, without considering the long-term consequences, or showing the need for this massive transfer of public resources to private hands. Far more coal and timber are on the block than industry can use. They will be used for private speculation instead of public benefit.

The lumber companies control more than a three-year supply of uncut timber on the public lands. Yet the Administration subsidizes even more sales—in virgin areas that might remain wilderness. Sixteen and one-half billion tons of coal are under lease to private industry—enough to last two centuries at the present rate of production. Yet the Administration, riding roughshod over land use plans the law requires, wants vastly expanded coal leasing.

In handing over the public resources to private interests, the Reagan Administration is devastatingly imprudent. More than that, it is betraying the agreement between the American people and their government—expressed in many laws—that the government will shield the public lands from abuse, develop commercial resources in a prudent balanced way, and protect noncommercial resources for lasting use.

The Administration's energy policy has been to eliminate virtually every program that provides direct benefits to individuals and small businesses seeking to conserve energy or use solar energy, while protecting billions of dollars in subsidies for nuclear power, synthetic fuels, and the oil industry.

This Administration is blind to the dangers of nuclear power. It has withdrawn safeguards against nuclear proliferation and, seeking a quick solution convenient for industry, has overridden a cautious process to deal with nuclear waste disposal. The Administration is considering the use of fuel from nuclear powerplants to make nuclear weapons, erasing the distinction drawn by President Eisenhower between Atoms for Peace and weapons for nuclear war.

The Reagan Administration's approach to the environment and natural resources, is not conservative; it is radical. Conservatives have recognized and helped to shape the essential role of government in conservation of the air, water and land we all share.

Without government intervention, for example, the company that voluntarily refrains from dumping wastes into a stream will be at a competitive disadvantage vis-a-vis another company that freely uses public waters as a private sewer. But the Administration sees government regulation of private pollution simply as an inconvenience for industry—a nuisance that should be reduced or eliminated.

Real free market principles are unpalatable to the Reaganite Sagebrush Rebels as well. They want the Federal Government to stop managing the public lands. So the Administration is turning over management of public rangeland to ranchers who pay grazing fees on public lands that are one-fifth the fees charged for private lands. This not only costs the nation money, but invites overgrazing, which has seriously damaged more than half the public range. Likewise, western farmers irrigating with water from federal dams pay one-fifth or less of the cost. Taxpayers pay the rest. The Administration has increased the budget for western water projects.

The problems of cleaning up pollution, managing public lands and water resources wisely, and encouraging the development of safe clean energy for the Nation's future cannot be resolved by private self interest alone. Government has a crucial role in protecting the natural world we all share—and on which our survival depends. That is why President Theodore Roosevelt built and protected our National Forest System in the early years of the century. It is why the Congress passed the Multiple Use Sustained Yield Act in 1960, the Wilderness Act in 1964, the Clean Air Act in 1970, the Clean Water Act in 1972, the National Forest Management, Hazardous Waste, and Toxic Substances Control Acts in 1976, the Surface Mining Act in 1977, and many more.
In 1969 the Congress declared a

> national policy which will encourage productive and enjoyable harmony between man and his environment; to promote efforts which will prevent or eliminate damage to the enviroment and biosphere and stimulate the health and welfare of man.
> (National Environmental Policy Act)

The Reagan Administration has turned its back on that goal, although the great laws Congress passed to fulfill it remain unchanged, and the public support that led to their enactment has not diminished but grown stronger.

We think the Administration's environmental policies have harmed the Nation, and that the harm grows steadily worse. We believe President Reagan should be called to task.

———————————

Pollution Control

A dozen years ago there was no national program to protect the public from the hazards of pollution. The federal laws that were on the books were weak and ineffective, and pollution was getting worse. The problem could be seen, felt, tasted, and smelled. Scientific evidence of the seriousness of environmental degradation mounted. Human health, basic biological systems, recreation, and the natural beauty of our land and waters were being destroyed.

The American public decided to put a stop to it. They demanded action and over the ensuing decade the Congress responded, passing by overwhelming, bipartisan votes a series of strong and innovative laws mandating federal action to protect the nation from poisons in the air, in the water, and on the land. Among the statutes enacted by Congress were:

Statute	Year Passed
Clean Air Act	1970
Clean Water Act	1972
Federal Insecticide, Fungicide, and Rodenticide Act	1972
Marine Resources, Research, and Sanctuaries Act	1972
Safe Drinking Water Act	1974
Solid Waste Disposal Act	1976
Toxic Substances Control Act	1976
Surface Mining Control and Reclamation Act	1977
Superfund	1980

These statutes were not the results of a brief fad or legislative caprice. They were major legislative initiatives enacted as a result of intense public concern with real problems that cause injury, sickness, death, and material devastation.

All of these laws, except for the Surface Mining Act, which is administered by the Office of Surface Mining in the Department of Interior, are the responsibility of the Environmental Protection Agency. EPA has been devastated by budget cuts. OSM staff is being decimated. Both agencies have cut back sharply on enforcement and drastically weakened regulations. Neither is doing the job Congress told it to do.

Air Pollution

The Clean Air Act, our flagship environmental law, is under attack. The Reagan Administration's legislative proposals, regulatory changes, and budget actions are crippling the nation's clean air program. They threaten to bring back an era of dangerous, damaging, dirty air.

Preamble

Air pollution can kill people and make them ill; it attacks the natural environment; it destroys property. Air pollution of various kinds causes or aggravates cancer, emphysema, bronchitis, heart disease, and other diseases. Acid rain destroys lakes and forests. Ozone causes billions of dollars in crop damage.

The clean air legislation passed a dozen years ago and strengthened five years ago requires EPA, with the help of the states, to clean up our air. For a decade there was progress. A start has been made on controlling pollution from automobiles, power-plants, smelters, refineries, and scores of other sources.

But enormous tasks remain: ensuring that existing nationwide health standards are met; regulating highly toxic pollutants, such as benzene and arsenic, that are still uncontrolled; controlling acid rain, and inspecting existing controls to ensure that they continue to work.

Charges

Instead of tackling these tasks, the Administration has marched backwards, abandoning the goal of clean air.

Weakening National Clean Air Standards. The Administration has proposed or supported amendments that would emasculate the Clean Air Act, has dragged its feet on issuing regulations the law requires, and has abolished or watered down existing regulations. Specifically, the Administration has called for amendments to the law that would

- Weaken health standards to cover only so-called "significant risks." This means abandoning protection of specially sensitive groups such as children, the elderly, people with heart and lung disease, and others. The Congress has already blocked this attack on health standards.
- Allow deadlines for attaining the air quality standards that protect the public health to slip from 1982 and 1987 to as late as 1993.
- Weaken auto emissions standards to allow more than a doubling of nitrogen oxide and carbon monoxide emissions—a change that would expose millions of people in as many as 16 major urban areas to continued unhealthy air.
- Cripple the requirement that new cars must meet emission standards before they are sold and the provisions for recall when they do not.
- Do away with requirements that, in polluted areas, new sources of pollution (such as powerplants, refineries, chemical plants) use the most effective pollution controls available.

- Repeal protection for areas with air that is still clean, thus allowing new polluters to locate there and use less than the most effective pollution control technology.
- Drastically weaken the carrot-and-stick provisions by which the federal government encourages states to adopt effective pollution control plans. Conscientious states that adopt good plans would be at the mercy of industries which threaten to move to states having weaker controls.
- Allow greatly increased pollution of the air in National Parks and wilderness areas.

While mounting this assault on the law itself, EPA has taken administrative action to undo existing clean air requirements and has failed to issue long-overdue regulations. Some of these changes are subtle but far-reaching. For example, the Clean Air Act program to meet health standards in polluted areas depends on review by the states of proposals to build new industrial sources of pollution. Illegally redefining the word "source," EPA has effectively exempted most new polluting industrial installations from state reviews.

EPA has also

- Proposed to weaken by up to 5 times heavy truck emission standards, even though the National Commission on Air Quality found that emissions from heavy trucks must be controlled if we are to meet national health standards for air quality.
- Proposed to weaken the automobile emissions standard for hydrocarbons to permit an increase of approximately 25 percent in hydrocarbon emissions (one of the constituents of photochemical smog).
- Proposed to weaken particulate emissions standards for diesel automobiles, the fastest growing and least controlled part of the automobile fleet.
- Failed to develop a particulate standard for diesel trucks.
- Failed to set required standards for industrial boilers and the most dangerous fine particulates.

The Administration has even proposed a retreat in control of lead, a pollutant which is especially dangerous to children. EPA itself has sponsored recent research which shows that even extremely low blood levels of lead affect the brain patterns of young children. Yet EPA has

- Developed proposals to allow increased use of lead in gasoline, thereby increasing human exposure, most significantly the exposure of inner city children. These proposals reverse a longstanding policy of the federal government to protect the health of the nation's children by rducing lead in the environment.

Failing to Act on Toxic Air Pollution. The Reagan Administraton's failure to move on toxic air pollution is especially threatening to millions of Americans who live in the shadow of chemical plants, coke ovens, and other factories which emit chemicals that can cause cancer and other deadly diseases. Recent research indicates that as much as 10 to 20 percent of lung cancer is due to air pollution. According to EPA, more than 300 plants in 39 states and territories emit large amounts of unregulated chemicals that are known or suspected to cause cancer or other serious diseases. Yet, after years of study, EPA has

- Failed to act on a list of 37 pollutants which threaten severe hazards to human health.
- Cut the budget for action on toxic air pollutants so sharply that it may be more than a decade before action on all these chemicals is even begun.

Failing to Act on Acid Rain. From West Virginia to Maine, aquatic life in lakes and streams is dying. Thousands of lakes in Minnesota alone are in jeopardy, and hundreds are dead as sulfur from industrial stacks creates acid precipitation. In many states, acid rain is blamed for damaging forests and farmland and eroding buildings. Acid rain is a disaster that is real and growing.

The Reagan Administration claims that more study is needed before acting to control acid rain. The Administration opposes strengthening the Clean Air Act to mandate control measures. The Administration even seeks to weaken controls in current law limiting sulphur emissions from new plants. Even the words "acid rain" are out of fashion at EPA: Mrs. Gorsuch prefers the expression "non-buffered precipitation."

The Reagan Administration wants changes in the Clean Air Act to

- Exempt new large industrial coal-fired boilers from requirements that assure that a minimum percentage of sulfur oxides are removed from their emissions.
- Allow extensions of deadlines for meeting sulfur dioxide standards, which would allow delays and relaxations until 1993.

The Reagan Administration is also, by administrative action, changing the sulfur emission levels allowed from existing sources. It has

- Increased authorized sulfur dioxide emissions by 1.5 million tons a year, a very significant amount. Nationwide SO_2 emissions are currently 29 million tons per year.

The Administration has also undone a requirement proposed two years ago that powerplants with tall smoke stacks must reduce their SO_2 emissions by 412,000 tons per year. Now, EPA

- Is requiring a reduction of only 166,800 tons per year of SO_2 emissions from powerplants with tall stacks. Since present SO_2 emissions from tall stacks are over 500,000 tons per year, this means that more than 333,000 tons will still be contributing to acid rain in states and nations downwind of the powerplants.

Although the Reagan Administration has provided extra funds for acid rain research ($22 million for FY

1983, up $12 million over FY 1982), the addition may have a fatal drawback if research is simply being "accelerated" for a 5–year study, instead of the 10–year study originally planned by EPA. Many of the most serious effects of acid rain do not show up in the first 5 years.

Decreasing Enforcement. EPA has reduced the credibility and effectiveness of the entire regulatory program by a sudden and radical decrease in enforcement actions.

- After a series of jolting reorganizations and sharp budget cuts, the cases filed in federal court have declined almost 75 percent since Mrs. Gorsuch took office.
- Gorsuch personally undercut enforcement when she agreed in a private meeting with corporate officials to look the other way when Thriftway Refiners violated the Clean Air Act by increasing the amount of lead they put in their gasoline.

Reducing Research and Monitoring. Budget cuts proposed by the Reagan Administration will cripple research for air programs. Overall, the Reagan budget for FY 1983 proposes cuts of 23 percent from the level of two years ago in air quality. Specifically, the Reagan Administration budget would

- Eliminate human epidemiological research on the health effects of air pollution.
- Cut clinical research on health effects by 50 percent, eliminating investigation of volatile organic chemicals.
- Cut research on hazardous air pollutants severely. The Agency will look at three hazardous pollutants in 1983. At that rate, it will take a decade to examine the list of substances deemed priority because of their threat to human health.

The budget for monitoring air programs and assisting states has also been drastically cut. The proposed Reagan budget for FY 1983 would

- Cut back by 40 percent monitoring of air quality to determine the levels and kinds of pollution already present in our air.
- Cut grants and technical assistance to state air programs by 30 percent, thus crippling state efforts to implement clean air requirements.

Hazardous Wastes

Millions of pounds of hazardous wastes are disposed of every day in America creating a terrible hazard to human health and our environment. During the past year the Reagan Administration has retreated from its responsibility to control hazardous dumps, clean up abandoned dumps, and prosecute illegal dumpers.

Preamble

In 1976, faced with overwhelming evidence that improper disposal of huge quantities of hazardous wastes was endangering the health of millions of Americans, Congress enacted the Resource Conservation and Recovery Act. The Act is designed to impose "cradle to grave" controls on "the treatment, storage, transportation, and disposal of hazardous wastes which have adverse effects on health and the environment . . .." Some 130 billion pounds of hazardous wastes are created each year. The goal of the hazardous waste law is to asure safe, tightly regulated handling and disposal of newly created wastes.

In 1980 Congress enacted legislation creating a "Superfund" to provide for cleanup of abandoned dumpsites and dangerous spills of toxic materials and to facilitate compensation of victims. The law imposes a tax on chemical producers, the revenues from which are placed in a fund to be used exclusively to clean up dumps and spills. The intent of Congress was that EPA aggressively seek to compel the responsible parties to complete the required cleanup and, failing that, use Superfund resources to do so.

Charges

From Love Canal tc the Valley of the Drums, the need for action is urgently apparent, yet during the past year EPA Administrator Anne Gorsuch and other officials of the Agency have made it unmistakably clear to polluters that hazardous waste controls are being undone.

Loosening Controls on Wastes.

- Shortly after Gorsuch took office, enforcement actions against illegal dumpers came to a halt. Enforcement staff are not even permitted to request information from suspected violators without top-level headquarters approval.
- Regulations to control incineration and surface storage of wastes, required by law to be issued by October 1978, were finally promulgated in January 1981. Gorsuch suspended implementation of these regulations for existing facilities in July 1981 and three months later proposed to withdraw them.
- The law also required regulations for the disposal of hazardous wastes in landfills to be issued by October 1978. EPA planned to get them out in 1981, but Gorsuch, ignoring an outstanding court order, has delayed them.

- Financial responsibility rules designed to assure that firms handling hazardous wastes have the necessary resources to protect the public and pay for damage or injuries resulting from spills, fires, and explosions were issued in January 1981. Gorsuch postponed these rules until April 1982 and has indicated she will suspend them altogether.
- In February 1981, without notice or public comment, Gorsuch suspended the prohibition against burial of liquid wastes in drums, the practice that created Love Canal. The public reaction to the suspension was so strong that EPA was forced to reimpose the ban. However, Gorsuch still proposes to permit the burial of liquid wastes in drums in 25 percent of the area of a landfill.
- In negotiations with industry attorneys in a pending litigation, EPA agreed to weaken permitting requirements for hazardous waste facilities. Facilities may now expand up to 50 percent without having to meet federal requirements.
- In March 1982 EPA deferred reporting requirements for hazardous waste generators. This action prevents citizens from obtaining information about local dumps, impedes enforcement, and deprives EPA of data needed to develop effective regulations.
- Gorsuch has proposed to slash the funds available to states and EPA Regional offices to implement and enforce hazardous waste requirements.

Delaying Implementation of Superfund.

- EPA has listed 115 of the most dangerous dumpsites around the nation. Legal action had been taken against 20 before Gorsuch took office. Since then the EPA enforcement section's major action has been to write letters to invite those responsible for creating the remaining dumps in to talk.
- The Superfund legislation required EPA to develop by June 1981 a National Contingency Plan to guide the search for and cleanup of dangerous sites and to prepare to respond to emergencies such as spills and explosions. A plan was finally proposed in March 1982. The proposal is so vague as to provide no guarantee that Superfund resources and authority will be used to clean up any site. The plan implies that EPA cares more about saving money than cleaning up sites to protect human health.
- In the first use of its Superfund authority, after a toxic dump site in Santa Fe Springs, California, caught fire in July 1981, top EPA officials quickly negotiated a private settlement with one of the responsible parties. The settlement limited the company's cleanup responsibility instead of requiring the cleanup to continue until the hazard was removed. It also *committed EPA to testify on behalf of the company in any subsequent lawsuit against it* arising from the dump and the fire.
- To direct the Superfund effort, Gorsuch has appointed Rita M. Lavelle, public affairs specialist for Aero Jet Liquid Rocket, a company that has, according to EPA, the third worst pollution record in the state of California, including a massive release of arsenic, phenols, sulfates, and a variety of carcinogens into unlined ponds.

The result of these actions is to increase the public health risk from hazardous wastes, as earth, air, surface and groundwater continue to be contaminated. The result is to undercut those responsible industries that have invested in safe waste disposal technologies, and to destroy the credibility EPA had sought to build, enabling it to convince communities across the nation they could safely allow new, regulated waste disposal facilities to be built. The Administration's retreat increases the likelihood of a new Love Canal.

Water Quality

The water that sustains our nation, our rivers, lakes, and underground aquifers, is threatened by sewage, sediments, and toxic chemicals. The law says the discharge of pollutants into the nation's waters must end by 1985. The Administration has chosen to abandon that goal and seeks to weaken the Clean Water Act.

Preamble

Water pollution affects us all. There are over 100,000 dischargers of industrial wastewater in the United States. Waters in every state in the nation are affected by industrial discharges.

Pollution from municipal sewage is even more prevalent. Runoff from city streets and rural lands adds still more pollution to streams, lakes, and coastal waters.

The water we drink may be unsafe. The General Accounting Office recently reported that there were 146,000 violations of safe drinking water standards across the nation in 1980 alone. Fisheries are being destroyed. Industrial discharges of kepone interrupted commercial fishing in Virginia's rich James River, and PCBs did the same to the Hudson River. Swimming, boating, and agriculture are affected.

The Clean Water Act, passed in 1972 and strengthened in 1977, directs the Environmental Protection Agency to develop and enforce rules to achieve the goal of "fishable and swimmable" waters by 1983 and the elimination of *all discharge* of pollutants by 1985. Both the Act and an outstanding court order require EPA to set rules to control the discharge of toxic water pollutants.

The Safe Drinking Water Act was passed in 1974 in response to evidence that the drinking water of many Americans was laced with dangerous chemicals ranging from asbestos to vinyl chloride. Ground water, which provides drinking water for half our citizens, has been contaminated in many places across the nation.

The Safe Drinking Water Act requires EPA to set minimum drinking water quality standards to protect human health and to establish rules to prevent the injection of contaminants into underground aquifers.

Progress has been made in improving water quality. Overall, further deterioration of surface waters seems to have ceased—which is progress, considering that our population and industrial activity are rising. There are numerous individual success stories. Rivers such as the Savannah, the Hudson, the Naugatuck, the Detroit, the Connecticut, and many others showed remarkable improvement. But control of toxic chemical pollution is still at a primitive stage. Ground water pollution is a special worry. It is not well monitored; yet there is mounting evidence that wells from Gray, Maine, to the San Gabriel Valley in California are being polluted by toxic chemicals. Once those chemicals get into ground water, they are terribly difficult and costly to remove.

A huge job remains to protect drinking water sources and achieve the "fishable and swimmable" goal.

Charges

The Reagan Administration has begun to implement policies that will not only halt progress but threatens to cause declines in water quality. Especially alarming is the Administration's retreat on control of toxic pollutants, which affect both surface and groundwaters and make water unfit for drinking and for aquatic life.

Retreating from Control of Toxics. During the past year, the Reagan Administration has

- Suspended the entire national pretreatment program for over one year and suspended critical portions of that program indefinitely. The purpose of the pretreatment program is to curtail toxic discharges into municipal treatment plants by over 60,000 industrial sources.
- Delayed the national program for setting toxic effluent limits on industrial discharges from tens of thousands of sources. Since January 1981, EPA has not issued a single regulation to limit toxic discharges, but has twice requested extensions in court-ordered deadlines. If granted, the delays would extend deadlines from 1981 to mid–1984—resulting in tens of millions of pounds of inadequately treated toxic chemical discharges yearly.
- Sought to escape from its court-ordered responsibility to clean up toxic "hot spots" of chemical pollution. Those are specific locations where even the best available technology will not be sufficient to protect human health and water quality. EPA has done virtually nothing to address this problem.
- Sought to escape from its court-ordered duty to identify dangerous toxic water pollutants that will not be controlled by regulations under development in the Agency.
- Proposed to amend the Clean Water Act by adding variances and deadline extensions to the Act's uniform national toxic cleanup requirements. Those amendments would seriously delay cleanup, add tremendous burdens to state permitting authorities, and ultimately fail to control toxic discharges because of lack of data and scientific methods.

- Decided not to impose new, stricter limits on toxic discharges in revised permits for thousands of industrial dischargers, who will thus be allowed delays in adopting best available technology. Instead of using the Agency's authority to issue, case by case, permits with stricter toxics limitations than those now in existence, EPA has decided to wait until nationally uniform standards are promulgated—even if it takes 2–3 more years to develop those rules. Of course, the permitting budget was cut accordingly.
- Weakened the standards designed to protect aquifers and eliminated protections against injections of hazardous wastes.
- Failed to develop permanent drinking water quality standards that protect against toxic organic contamination.

Relaxing Other Water Quality Requirements. The Reagan Administration also has

- Developed a regulation (soon to be proposed) that would significantly relax treatment requirements for municipalities. EPA plans to "redefine" the requirement of secondary treatment so that the horrible noncompliance rate by cities suddenly will disappear.
- Developed a regulation (soon to be proposed) that would assist those states wishing to use their waterways for waste transport. In effect, the regulation would encourage states to downgrade their water quality standards, instead of enforcing the Act's national goal of fishable, swimmable water quality.

Toxic Substances

Progress in controlling toxic chemicals that threaten public health and the environment has been disappointingly slow. Now even the little that has been achieved is unravelling. Under the Reagan Administration, EPA's attention is focused on easing requirements on industry, not on increasing protection for the public.

Preamble

Industrial chemicals are pervasive in our world. There are over 40,000 chemicals produced or used in the United States. Ten to twenty new chemical compounds enter the stream of commerce every week. Manmade chemicals are a part of virtually all commercial products used today.

Many chemicals are benign, but some are extraordinarily dangerous, even in tiny quantities. Some cause cancer, birth defects, heart and lung disease, and a host of other ailments. Because the damage they do may take years, even decades, to show up in humans, people often suffer long exposure to hazardous chemicals before their effects are fully known. Vinyl chloride was widely used for many years—despite laboratory tests showing it caused cancer in animals—before we learned that it causes human cancer. Asbestos was used in talcum powder, wallboard, hair dryers, brake linings, and many other products for decades before epidemiological studies definitively showed it is a human carcinogen. Animal studies implicating asbestos as a carcinogen had been done much earlier.

Because of these tragedies in which humans have served as guinea pigs, and because of the proven ability of positive animal testing to predict effects in humans, the federal government established cancer policies which treat animal data as a sufficient basis for regulation. This established policy rejects the view that human evidence ("counting dead bodies") is necessary to initiate protective regulation.

The Toxic Substances Control Act (TSCA) was enacted in 1976 to assure that "innovation and commerce in chemical substances and mixtures do not present an unreasonable risk of injury to health or the environment." TSCA authorizes EPA to require testing of certain existing chemicals to determine whether they are hazardous; to restrict or prohibit the manufacture of chemicals that pose an unreasonable risk to human health; and to screen new chemicals to identify potential "bad actors" before, rather than long after, human beings are exposed to them.

TSCA is a complicated law, and the Carter Administration moved very slowly in carrying it out. It did make a useful beginning, preparing several rules that require manufacturers to test highly suspicious chemicals and proposing quality standards for the data industry submits.

Charges

The Reagan Administration has cancelled the slow progress made so far under TSCA to identify and control toxic chemicals. It has made a dangerous decision, in defiance of the overwhelming weight of scientific opinion, not to accept animal test data alone as presumptive evidence that a chemical is a human carcinogen. It is negotiating with industry on controversial chemicals behind closed doors, with the public and impartial scientists excluded. It has failed to finalize rules that require manufacturers to test priority chemicals that are already in use and is withdrawing proposed testing standards. It is relying instead on "voluntary" compliance by industry. It is retreating on protection against asbestos, a known dangerous substance.

Rejecting A Protective Cancer Policy. Long-term testing using laboratory animals is a scientifically sound way of identifying likely human carcinogens. The other generally accepted approach is through epidemiological studies comparing people exposed to a possible carcinogen with those who are not exposed.

Epidemiological studies are always costly, are usually relatively insensitive, and are often difficult or impossible to do. Many cancers do not show up until years after the exposure; most people are exposed to a great many carcinogens during their lives, which makes it hard to isolate the effect of one substance; and it is often difficult to find a suitable

group of people who have not been exposed to particular substances, for comparison with others who have been. Animal tests, on the other hand, can be done under controlled conditions and can provide clearcut results. The International Agency for Research on Cancer, a federal interagency panel, and many other scientific groups have recommended that carcinogens identified in well-conducted animal tests be treated as potential human carcinogens. Up until now, government agencies have done so. A number of pesticides and carcinogens found in the workplace have been regulated on that basis.

President Reagan's EPA has suddenly reversed the established policy.

● Dr. John Todhunter, the new EPA Assistant Administrator for Toxics, decided that results of valid animal tests of formaldehyde, plus the fact of widespread human exposure, were not a sufficient basis for protective action. This decision flies in the face of the scientific consensus. It reverses EPA's former prudent approach of assessing and regulating cancer risks *before* they affect human beings.

Consulting Privately with Industry. In the fall of 1980 EPA received the results of animal experiments indicating that formaldehyde and di(2–ethylhexyl)phthalate (DEHP), both widely used chemicals, are carcinogens. Formaldehyde is used in plywood, particle board, home insulation, furniture, and fabrics, cosmetics, and toothpaste. DEHP is used in hundreds of plastic products, including building materials, food wrappers, toys, rubber baby pants, and milking machine hoses. After receiving the animal data, the staff of EPA recommended formal proceedings to determine the extent of the risk to human health, and action by EPA to limit human exposure.

Instead, the new leaders at EPA

● Convened a series of private meetings with industry—the Formaldehyde Institute, the Chemical Manufacturer's Association, Exxon, and others—to evaluate the studies and the risk of the substances.
● Did not notify or invite the public, environmentalists who had formally requested action on formaldehyde and DEHP, or even some of EPA's top cancer experts.
● After the meetings, rejected the prior staff recommendations and refused to institute proceedings (priority assessment) on the two chemicals.

Later, in a separate action, the Consumer Product Safety Commission concluded that the evidence against formaldehyde was compelling and banned urea formaldehyde foam insulation.

Relying on Voluntary Compliance by Industry. The Toxic Substances Control Act requires EPA to set rules for industry to test the safety of existing chemicals that a committee of experts concludes may pose a risk of cancer or injury to health or the environment. A 1981 court order requires EPA to issue test rules or explain why testing is unnecessary for 37 priority chemicals in the next two years. Instead of moving ahead with this critical task, EPA has

- Failed to issue pending test rules and delayed action on additional rules.
- Cut back sharply on resources necessary to develop test rules.
- Engaged in negotiations with industry to substitute "voluntary" testing for legal requirements.

Under another section of TSCA, the manufacturer of a new chemical must give EPA advance notice so that EPA can review the data available on potential hazards to human health. In 1982, EPA will receive 500 to 1000 such notices. EPA has:

- Failed to finalize the program for new chemical reporting.
- Cut back review staff, so that most notices of new chemical manufacture will receive only rubber-stamp review.
- Retreated from efforts to set minimum standards for data to be submitted by the manufacturers of new chemicals.
- Begun developing a rule at the request of the Chemical Manufacturers Association to exempt an estimated 75 percent of new chemicals from the notice requirement.

Retreating on Control of Known Dangerous Substances. Asbestos fibers cause asbestosis (fibrosis of the lungs), cancer of the lungs and digestive tract, and mesothelioma. Despite the proven health hazards of asbestos, the new EPA has

- Cut back on efforts to identify schools in which building materials expose children to asbestos.
- Weakened the warning on asbestos in schools approved by its own Science Advisory Committee.

At least 3 million students and 250,000 teachers may be affected by the retreat from protection against asbestos in schools.

Polychlorinated biphenyls (PCBs) are extremely toxic industrial chemicals. They have been widely used in electrical transformers, and they are pervasive in our environment. They are present in human breast milk and adipose tissue at toxicologically significant levels. PCB contamination has closed several rivers to fishing. In 1979 the leakage of 200 gallons of PCBs from a single transformer at the Pierce Packing Plant in Billings, Montana contaminated feed and food in 19 states and required the destruction of millions of dollars worth of contaminated livestock and food. Congress included in TSCA a provision that EPA ban the use of PCBs.

Under the Carter Administration, EPA issued regulations exempting the vast majority of PCBs in use from the ban. These regulations were overturned in court. Now, EPA is studying the question of new regulations, but has reduced the resources available to carry out the Congressional mandate.

Coal Mining

Coal mining imposed heavy social and environmental costs on the public for years in many areas of the country. Especially in Appalachia, mining has ruinously affected the quality of community life. In 1977 Congress passed the Surface Mining Control and Reclamation Act to end the abuse of the environment and the threats to human safety caused by mining. From the moment he took office, Secretary of the Interior James Watt has worked diligently to gut the protections afforded by the Act.

Preamble

Each week a thousand acres of land are disturbed by surface mining for coal in the United States. Mining has ruined more than ten thousand miles of streams through acid drainage or siltation. Thousands of miles of highwalls standing above lands gouged by stripmining are unreclaimed. Thousands of acres of prime farmland have been destroyed in the Midwest. A study in the mid–1970s concluded that it would cost over ten billion dollars to partially repair the damage already done. Mining since then has caused much additional damage.

Coal mining causes massive damage in different ways in different parts of the country. In the Eastern coalfields, where spoil is still pushed over mountainsides, the result is often landslides, erosion, rubble-clogged streams, and flooding. Unstable highwalls crumble and erode, ruining drainage patterns and adding to water pollution. Erosion increases dramatically when protective vegetative cover is removed and the soil is not stabilized. Suspended sediment concentration in small Appalachian streams that drain stripmining areas has increased 100 times over that of streams in undisturbed forest lands. To this day, coal mining in Appalachia often results in a legacy of polluted streams below mountainsides left treacherously unstable.

As devastating as the mining has been to the environment, the impact on the politically disenfranchised citizens of Appalachia has been greater. More than any other environmental law, the Surface Mining Act is intended to redress the grievances of the people of Appalachia whose communities bear the results of mining abuses—mudslides that destroy homes and even lives, the ruin of local streams, and the destruction of natural beauty.

In the Midwest, mining has injured agricultural lands that are among the most productive in the world. The Surface Mining Act includes specific provisions to provide for protection of prime farmland soils and aquifers.

In the Western coalfields, mining occurs in arid or semi-arid areas. In arid climates, the land's protective vegetative cover is fragile. Once it has been disturbed by mining, erosion increases dramatically. Most importantly, in areas with little rainfall, restoration of vegetative cover is almost impossible without irrigation.

In many of the Western coalfields, stripmining

interferes with ground water aquifers, changing flow patterns and leaving some parts of the aquifer without water. Wells dry up or are contaminated, affecting irrigation on nearby ranches and farms.

Charges

Shortly after Secretary Watt took office, he announced plans to rewrite the coal mining regulatory program to make it "less burdensome" for coal companies. He has initiated 45 separate changes that weaken every aspect of the program.

Undoing Protective Rules. The Reagan Administration has withdrawn some of the most important regulations implementing standards contained in the law to protect the environment from coal mining.

- Without notice or comment, Watt withdrew final regulations intended to protect the nation's prime farmlands from the ravages of stripmining.
- The Office of Surface Mining adopted a policy of "paying for highwalls" by which coal operators could evade the most important performance standard in the Act—return of land after mining to approximate original contour—and save millions of dollars in operating costs by paying a fine of a few thousand dollars.
- Watt weakened the standards for approval of state stripmine programs. Using the new weaker standards, he is approving state programs which will not protect the environment as Congress intended.

The Administration has proposed to

- Eliminate the requirement that mining operators control dust created by mining and coal handling.
- Broaden the exemption from environmental rules for small mines.

Gutting Inspections and Enforcement.

- The Administration is reducing the number of OSM field inspectors from 145 to 69. Last year Congress refused to allow the reduction. Watt is proposing it again for FY 1983.
- The Office of Surface Mining has proposed the elimination of significant enforcement powers for federal inspectors, thus preventing any effective oversight of state performance.
- Enforcement actions against coal operators have decreased by over 30 percent.
- The Office of Surface Mining has failed to assess and collect over $40 million in mandatory fines owed the government by coal operators.

Evading Federal Responsibilities.

- Watt has proposed to relinquish to the states essential regulatory functions that the law mandates be shared by the federal government and the states.
- The Office of Surface Mining has decided to essentially ignore the Act's requirement to issue new permits for every coal mine in the United States (over 17,000) as permanent regulations take effect over the next year.

Limiting Public Participation.

- The Administration has proposed to curtail the rights of citizens to propose lands as unsuitable for mining, to participate in permit reviews, and to play a role in other aspects of the regulatory program.

The inevitable result of Mr. Watt's policies will be to increase the ravages caused by stripmining in the form of polluted streams, unreclaimed land, loss of wildlife resources, erosion, the loss of prime farmland, and the degradation of the quality of life of the citizens in coal producing areas.

On December 18, 1981, a coal waste pile collapsed, sending sludge and other debris down a mountain, killing one elderly woman and routing more than a hundred persons from their homes in Harlan County, Kentucky. The elderly woman who died had complained repeatedly to federal officials about the unsafe activities of the mining company. Prior to the devastation, the Office of Surface Mining had sharply cut inspectors and enforcement actions.

The Federal Public Lands and Natural Resources

Some 500 million acres of federal public land owned by all Americans—190 million in the National Forests and 328 million under the Bureau of Land Management—are required to be managed, under law, for multiple use, sustained yield of renewable resources, and long-term conservation. The Reagan Administration has tilted management away from conservation toward rapid development and control by private interests.

By accelerating the leasing of oil, gas, and coal on federal lands, without regard for demand and at royalty rates that are too low, the Reagan Administration is conducting a giveaway of the resources that belong to the nation.

It continues to subsidize the western livestock industry through grazing fees far below market value. It has adopted a new "Grazing Management Policy" and has proposed regulation changes that will allow ranchers to dominate—practically dictate—rangeland decisions. While passing effective control of publicly owned range to the livestock operators, the Administration is practically closing the door on government programs to benefit fish and wildlife and public recreation.

Ignoring both market realities and multiple use principles, President Reagan's Department of Agriculture has forced upon the Forest Service a policy of selling timber faster than it grows and of cutting timber on steep and arid lands where it should not be cut—all at an economic loss to the public, and damaging to wildlife, recreation, and watershed values. The Reagan policy not only subsidizes the timber industry, but gives it greater control over the National Forests.

The Administration set out to open the National Wilderness Preservation System to oil and gas drilling and mining—a goal blocked by Congress. Recently, proclaiming an intent to "protect" the wilderness areas, Secretary of the Interior James Watt recommended legislation that would open all wilderness to energy and minerals development after the year 2000. The Administration has signalled its clear intent to open to development lands being studied for wilderness designation, and to make certain there are no further major additions to the system.

Mr. Reagan himself has endorsed the goals of the "Sagebrush Rebellion" whose leaders have tried to get federal public lands turned over to the states and eventually to private ownership. Now the Administration has proposed to "privatize" large areas of National Forests and BLM lands by selling them to private interests.

Two other major systems of federal public lands, the National Parks and the National Wildlife Refuges, are endangered by this Administration. While vowing to rehabilitate National Parks, Secretary Watt has systematically reduced the capability of the Park Service by cutting staff and funds for operations. He has tried to block further land acquisitions for the National Park System.

Likewise, he has tried to stop acquisition of National Wildlife Refuges, and has curtailed important activities of the Fish and Wildlife Service. His particular target for decimation has been the Endangered Species Program.

National Forests

Eighty years ago, President Theodore Roosevelt built the National Forest System on a strong foundation of conservation principles. The Reagan Administration is discarding this heritage. It is evading the express mandate of federal law to manage National Forests for many purposes, commercial and noncommercial. It is proposing an unbalanced, economically unsound, environmentally damaging program that would serve private timber and mining interests at the expense of broader public benefits.

Preamble

The conservation movement in this country had its origin in forest protection. Toward the end of the last century, rapacious "cut and run" commercial timbering left a legacy of scarred landscapes, erosion and floods. In response, publicly owned national forest reserves were established in 1891, and were greatly expanded and strengthened ten years later by President Theodore Roosevelt.

Congress has many times reaffirmed and strengthened the Roosevelt conservation policy for the National Forests. It has established a philosophy of management for sustained yield and multiple uses—outdoor recreation, range, timber, watershed, wilderness, and fish and wildlife habitat. In recent years, the Forest and Rangeland Renewable Resources Planning Act of 1974 created a long-term planning process to achieve those goals. Congress spelled out forest management guidance in more detail in the National Forest Management Act of 1976. With that law, Congress meant to stop abuses caused by dominant use of national forests for timber production, and to require greater attention by federal forest managers to resource protection and noncommodity uses.

Charges

The Reagan Administration is offering the timber industry a $150 million-a-year subsidy for a timber sale that is too big, makes no sense economically, and threatens serious harm to the environment. The Administration's policy is to impose commercial resource extraction as the dominant use of the National Forests. It wants to undo years of professional planning for wise, balanced management of our National Forests—planning based on wide public participation and under standards prescribed by law. Moreover, President Reagan has put in charge of the nation's publicly owned forests a former timber industry executive and outspoken advocate of the industry's interests.

Subsidizing the Timber Industry. Despite a current low demand for timber and an all-time high backlog of sold but uncut timber in the National Forests, the Reagan Administration proposes to increase timber sales dramatically.

• The Reagan budget requests a timber sale from the National Forests of 12.3 billion board feet for FY 1983. That is 4 billion board feet higher than the amount cut last year. The excessive FY 1983 sale is planned despite the depressed housing industry and a record high backlog of approximately 34 billion board feet. The backlog amounts to more than three years' worth of average timber sales from the National Forests.

• The proposed timber sale conceals at least a $150 million subsidy. The sale will cost the U.S. Treasury $665 million (mostly for road construction). The Forest Service has in the past acknowledged that 22 percent of its timber sales are below cost. If these subsidized sales were eliminated, the sale could be reduced to a more realistic 9.6 billion board feet. Savings to the taxpayers would be $150 million.

• The proposed sale is environmentally unsound. The budget for the sale shows $585 million for road building, $200 million more than in 1982. As the Reagan budget itself explains, the sharply higher cost is for roads in "difficult terrain" with "access problems." Forest Service research shows road construction is the prime cause of soil erosion, silting of streams, and damage to trout fisheries in the National Forests. Those problems are doubly acute in "difficult terrain."

• Some of the sales would be made in virgin areas of the National Forests that have never before had roads. Opening roads into them would remove them forever from possible designation as wilderness.

Federal sales below cost do not necessarily increase national supplies. In fact, they can unfairly compete with production for profit on private lands and discourage investments there.

Making Resource Extraction the Dominant Use. The wasteful expenditures for roads and subsidized timber sales robs the Forest Service of funds needed for other multiple use responsibilities. The Administration's FY 1983 budget request for the Forest Service slashes funds for recreation, fish and wildlife, and watershed protection, while sharply increasing support for timber and mineral activities.

The Forest Service's 1980 long-term program was drawn up by professionals under the Resources Planning Act and was adopted by Congress, with some revision, in 1980. This current, Congressionally approved RPA Program gives balanced consideration to all the resources of the National Forests. The Reagan FY 1983 budget proposal skews the Forest Service's program planning out of all proportion. It meets or exceeds the goals for timber sales, mineral development, and livestock grazing, but cuts fish and wildlife management goals by 64 percent, trail construction by 90 percent, and soil and water protection by 99 percent.

Further examples are:

• The Reagan FY 1983 budget would cut trail maintenance by 30 percent from 1982 levels. Already, in the 1982 budget, maintenance was abandoned for 10,000 miles of the 100,000-mile trail system in National Forests. The further cut would mean that another 30,000 miles would be allowed to deteriorate.

• No allowance is made in the FY 1983 Reagan budget for wildlife habitat protection, except in timber sale areas.

The Osceola National Forest in Florida is a victim of the Reagan Administration's policy to sacrifice multiple uses of the public forests to resource extraction.

• After almost 10 years of opposing the issuance of leases for open pit mining of phosphate in the Osceola National Forest because of severe adverse impacts on wildlife, recreation, and air and water resources, the Department of the Interior and EPA have recently reversed their position. The Interior Department, which has the authority to issue those leases under the Mineral Leasing Act of 1920, is apparently disregarding existing regulations, as well as a 1981 solicitor's opinion, in processing the pending lease applications.

Frustrating the Reforms Imposed by Law. Changes proposed by the Reagan Administration in forest planning regulations are of dubious legality and will frustrate the reforms Congress called for in the National Forest Management Act. Regulations under the Act had been adopted in final form in 1979, after three laborious years of drafting, public comments, redrafting, and reaching a workable compromise among the many interests using the National Forests. Discarding that carefully crafted compromise, the Reagan Administration would

• Abandon sustained yield management to allow rapid increases in cutting the old, pristine forests in the Pacific Northwest. The law requires that departures from sustained yield management must be carefully controlled exceptions. Under the proposed changes, the exceptions would become the rule. The Chief of the Forest Service would no longer have to personally approve departures from the sustained yield principle. In fact, individual forest supervisors would be *required* to consider departures from the principle in a broad range of circumstances—which virtually guarantees the liquidation of the forests.

- Require strict cost-benefit tests to be applied to non-commodity public uses of the forests but, ironically, allow timber production even from areas where the timber industry would never invest because production there is not economically sound. The effect will be to water down the protection of environmentally fragile areas from road construction and logging.
- Arbitrarily restrict consideration of especially scenic or ecologically valuable lands for wilderness designation.
- Eliminate portions of the regulations designed to encourage public participation in the forest planning process.
- Eliminate integrated pest management (IPM) as the principle for dealing with pests in National Forests. IPM involves minimal use of environmentally harmful chemical pesticides.
- Remove the requirement to maintain or improve habitat for valuable species such as trout or elk.

These changes come from the office of Assistant Secretary of Agriculture John B. Crowell. He was formerly general counsel of the Louisiana-Pacific timber firm, one of the largest timber cutters on federal lands. He was also chairman of a timber industry panel when the original regulations were developed. His chief deputy also comes from the timber industry. The proposed changes in regulations adopt almost exactly the positions the timber industry took as the regulations were being developed.

BLM Lands Management

The 328 million acres of public lands under the care of the Bureau of Land Management must be managed, under the law, for multiple use and long-term conservation. The Reagan Administration has tilted management of BLM lands toward resource development by private interests at the expense of resource conservation, and has cut the public out of the planning process.

Preamble

A century ago, federal policy was to give away the federally owned public lands and their resources to private interests. Gradually, the public and the Congress came to a consensus that the lands should be managed for a broad array of public interests, including both commercial resource development and noncommercial uses.

In 1976 Congress passed the Federal Land Policy and Management Act—the long awaited Bureau of Lands Management Organic Act. It directed BLM, the nation's largest landowner, to manage its lands for multiple resource use and sustained yield, so as to protect their scientific, scenic, historical, ecological, environmental, air and atmospheric, water resource, and archaeological values. The law calls for prompt development of land use plans with public involvement.

Charges

Sacrificing Conservation for Resource Exploitation. Secretary of the Interior James Watt has poured money and staff into accelerated energy development on the public lands, while taking them away from renewable resource management and environmental protection. For the Bureau of Land Management, Watt has

- Sharply increased staff for onshore and offshore oil and gas leasing—40 new full-time positions in FY 1982 and 144 more proposed in FY 1983.
- Cut 130 full-time staff in FY 1982, with 195 further staff cuts scheduled in FY 1983, for resource inventories and environental analyses in forest, range, recreation, wildlife habitat, and soil, water, and air management. This despite the increased need for analyzing the impacts of stepped-up oil and gas activities.
- Cut 28 positions for technical and environmental studies of coal development, while proposing the sale of 2.4 billion tons of federally owned coal in the Powder River Basin—five times larger than any sale in history—and seeking to speed up the leasing of publicly owned coal elsewhere.
- Cut the BLM planning budget by 48 percent. BLM planners are those who identify and try to reconcile conflicts among competing uses of the public lands. This cut could invite litigation, delay even well-conceived development, and impose extra costs on industry.

Historically, the staff and resources devoted to conservation on the public lands has closely matched the resources committed to resource development. The Reagan Administration is destroying the balance. The tilt is unprecedented and threatens serious long-term harm to the environmental quality and ecological health of the public lands.

Cutting the Public Out of BLM Planning. Claiming that many of the public participation rules under the Federal Land Policy and Management Act were "burdensome and unnecessary," the BLM has not only cut the public out of the planning but has trivialized the plans themselves. In proposed amendments to the FLPMA regulations, BLM would

- Make proposed planning criteria available only on request, rather than publishing them for comment.
- No longer require that changes in criteria be made public.
- Select the land use plan on the basis of internal agency "guidance" (not subject to public review),

rather than the planning criteria.
- Allow BLM managers to take any action that does not "clearly contradict the land use plan," whereas previously such actions were to be "clearly consistent" with the plans.

The result of these changes would be to cut the connections between the criteria and the plans, between the plans and the real decisions, and between the public and the whole process. The last change would all but eliminate judicial review of planning decisions, since the difficulties of proving that an action "clearly contradicts" a land use plan would be insurmountable.

In short, decisions on the use of the public lands will be made behind closed doors by Interior Department officials unwilling to subject those decisions to the light of public review.

The Sagebrush Rebellion

The Reagan Administration is satisfying some of the demands of the "Sagebrush Rebels" by dropping conservation goals in managing western public lands. The Administration also proposes to reduce its huge budget deficits by selling off National Forest and other public lands. This one-time profit taking would deprive the nation forever of revenue-producing resources, would end multiple use management and conservation of important national lands, and would violate the intent of laws governing the public lands.

Preamble

The Federal Land Policy and Management Act of 1976 gave BLM real authority for the first time in its history. The next year the Surface Mining Act became law. Ranchers, miners, offroad vehicle users, and others who had been accustomed to doing as they pleased on the public lands discovered they could no longer do so. Led by livestock interests, they launched a political campaign that came to be known as the Sagebrush Rebellion. Its goal was to seize the federal public lands (including the National Forests) from public ownership, turn them over to the states, and move them into private ownership or private control.

Six western states, led by Nevada, laid claim to federal lands in court. None have won their cases. Some Western Congressmen introduced legislation to give the public lands to the states but because of popular opposition they received little serious attention.

Charges

Campaigning for President, Ronald Reagan said in Salt Lake City: "I am a Sagebrush Rebel." Once elected, he

- Appointed another self-professed Sagebrush Rebel Secretary of the Interior and another, Colorado rancher Robert Burford, to head the Bureau of Land Management.

Though court suits and legislation inspired by the Sagebrush Rebellion have failed, the Reagan Administration has satisfied some of its aims piecemeal. The Administration has

- Crippled BLM's land use planning (see BLM Lands Management).
- Changed grazing policy to put ranchers back in charge of the public range (see Grazing).
- Emasculated the Office of Surface Mining, upset regulations, and failed to enforce the law (see Coal Mining).
- Weakened regulations to control surface damage at mines and drilling sites.
- Ignored the BLM regulations governing use of offroad vehicles on the public lands. Secretary of the Interior Watt has tried—unsuccessfully so far—to get President Reagan to rescind the Nixon and Carter Executive Orders requiring control of ORV damage on the public lands.
- Invited the minerals industry to enter wilderness areas (see Wilderness).

The Administration now proposes to reduce its alarming budget deficit by selling off public lands—"privatize them," in the words of a White House economic advisor. The Administration plans to

- Sell $17 billion worth of National Forest and BLM lands over five years. This could amount to 35 million acres. The sale would deprive the nation of valuable revenue-producing resources (timber, minerals, range) and put an end to multiple use and environmentally protective management of those lands.

Grazing

The public range has been seriously damaged by more than a century's overgrazing. The Reagan Administration's remedy is to spend federal money improving a part of the public range, and turn the improved portion over to private ranchers for their dominant use and control.

Preamble

Of the 328 million acres (including land in Alaska) managed by BLM, about 170 million acres are classified as "rangelands" for livestock grazing. Some 55 percent of this land is officially described as in "low or moderately low" condition. "Low" means that soil and vegetation meet 20 percent or less of the potential of the site. The federally owned rangelands have been abused primarily by overgrazing in the past; and overgrazing is still going on.

A major purpose of the land use plans required by the Federal Land Policy and Management Act is to protect and restore grazing lands—not only for the use of livestock, but also for the elk herds, mule deer, bighorn sheep, and pronghorn antelope that depend on the public lands for forage. Another important reason for restoring the Western grasslands is to control water and wind erosion, thus helping to reverse conditions that are threatening to create a new Dust Bowl.

Charges

Allowing Rangeland to Deteriorate and Ranchers to Dominate Rangeland Use. Rather than trying to heal the wounds caused by overgrazing, the Reagan Administration wants to reduce drastically federal regulation of livestock grazing on the public lands.

● Watt has cut 60 staff positions and $3.8 million from grazing management activities in the FY 1983 budget.

Whatever funds are available for range improvement would go into land that is set aside mainly for production of red meat. Needs of wildlife and other non-commercial values would be all but ignored.

The new BLM grazing policy

● Divides rangeland into "custodial," "maintenance," and "improvement" categories, with funds targeted to the last category with the principal objective of yielding "maximum economic return." The policy appears to contradict FLPMA's multiple use mandate, which requires that consideration be given to the relative value of resources and not necessarily to the combination of uses that will give the greatest economic return or the greatest economic output.
● Separates grazing decisions from overall land use planning. It demonstrates the effect (prematurely since the rules have not yet been finally changed) of dropping the requirement that management decisions shall be *consistent* with land use plans.

The Administration has made no effort to stop the gross subsidies of livestock grazing on the public lands. The public land grazing fee in 1982 will be $1.86 per animal unit month (which is the grazing of one cow or five sheep in one month). Comparable private grazing lease rates are $8.83. The artificially cheap price for grazing on the public lands invites the overgrazing which has badly damaged so much of the public land.

National Parks

For 110 years the National Park System has grown with the nation. It has offered the enjoyment of scenery, wildlife, and "natural wonders" to increasing numbers of Americans, while conserving those resources for future generations. The Reagan Administration has halted the park system's growth and is ignoring threats to the parks from air and water pollution and development on adjacent land. Its policies threaten the unique values that the park system is meant to preserve.

Preamble

The National Park System Organic Act of 1916 says the purpose of the parks is "to conserve the scenery and the natural and historic objects and the wildlife . . . and to provide for the enjoyment of the same in such manner . . . as will leave them unimpaired for the enjoyment of future generations." Today the system includes not only the great old parks like Yellowstone and Yosemite, but also national seashores and recreation areas, monuments, historic sites, sites for the performing arts, scenic rivers and trails, and open spaces in the nation's capital.

In 1980, about one American in four visited a National Park unit. Visits to parks are multiplying rapidly, reaching 300 million in 1980—ten times the number of visits in 1950 and 300 times the number in 1930.

For more than a century, Congress has continually added to the park system by designating suitable lands from the public domain and by buying privately held land. In 1965, Congress created the Land and Water Conservation Fund, which receives income mainly from offshore oil and gas leasing. Congress is authorized to appropriate up to $900 million a year from the Fund to buy land for national parks, wildlife refuges and forests and to help states plan, purchase, and develop state parks. In that way, Congress provided that a modest share of the offshore oil and gas revenues (which totalled $9.8 billion in 1981) will be used to conserve irreplaceable natural landscapes, historic places, and important recreation areas.

Charges

Stopping Growth of the Park System. The Reagan Administration opposes buying parkland already authorized by Congress, creating new parks, helping states buy and develop parks, and supporting urban parks in any way.

● Shortly after taking office, Secretary of the Interior James Watt imposed a complete moratorium on all federal land purchases from the Land and Water Conservation Fund. He also stopped all federal grants from the Fund to states. He stated publicly that he believes most "truly unique" park areas have already been acquired, and that the federal government should not provide urban or regional parks. In other words, the Administration policy is that the park system need grow no further.

- In the FY 1982 budget request for the National Park Service, Secretary Watt asked for approximately $39 million from the Land and Water Conservation Fund for acquisition of federal parkland. Those funds were to cover only court awards and administrative costs for purchases already in progress. That amount compares with an average appropriation of about $550 million for each of the previous five years. Rejecting Watt's policy, Congress actually appropriated $150 million in FY 1982 for federal parkland acquisition.
- Secretary Watt asked for no money for state grants in FY1982 and 1983. Congress appropriated none in FY1982, but made it clear the moratorium was for one year only.

The Reagan Administration's total cutoff of funds for parkland is a radical departure from policies over 100 years old. It violates the intent of Congress in creating the Land and Water Conservation Fund. The nation's growing population will have to share a fixed number of ever more heavily used National Parks. Critical lands needed to protect unique natural areas or to buffer existing parks against development will be lost or will have to be purchased later at much higher prices. There are now approximately 65 National Park units in 32 states for which land acquisition (presently valued at more than $1 billion) has been authorized by Congress but not completed. Among the critical lands are the Appalachian Trail corridor, the Channel Islands off California, the Big Cypress Swamp in Florida, and the Santa Monica Mountain National Recreation Area near Los Angeles.

Ignoring Threats to the Parks. Secretary Watt's announced policy for the National Park System is to emphasize restoration, improvement, and maintenance of facilities in existing parks, rather than to continue to acquire land. He has asked Congress to amend the Land and Water Conservation Act to allow the Fund to be used for maintenance purposes. He has asked for $105 million for restoration and maintenance of park facilities in FY 1983.

Maintaining park facilities to meet health and safety standards is important. However, Secretary Watt's priorities go in the wrong direction.

- The Watt proposal to dip into the Land and Water Conservation Fund for maintenance would rob it of money needed for buying additional parklands.
- The maintenance funds Secretary Watt is seeking for FY 1983 would go almost entirely to refurbishing roads, bridges, buildings, sewers, and park facilities, rather than for protection of the irreplaceable natural resources which are the park system's reason for existence. Indeed, emphasis on improvement of roads and park facilities may promote further heavy use of much-visited parks and add to the wear and tear on natural resources. The result could be first-rate plumbing and roads in a second-rate park system.

The most immediate and serious threat to the national parks is pollution from internal and external sources. In a 1980 report to the Congress, the National Park Service listed the threats which are causing severe degradation of park resources. Approximately 60 percent of the parks reported significant threats to scenic resources. Air and fresh-water quality, mammals and plants were reported threatened in about 40 percent of the parks. The Park Service staff has singled out specific threats to the natural resources of individual parks and has proposed research and protection measures. Yet Secretary Watt has asked for minimal funds to mitigate existing resource damage and to prevent new threats from developing.

In fact, the Administration has taken actions which increase pollution and other threats to the parks.

- The Administration has proposed amendments to the Clean Air Act that would eliminate protection of air quality and scenic vistas in national parks and wilderness areas. Air pollution, reduced visibility, and a closing in of vistas is already a major problem in national parks that are near large powerplants. For example, the Four Corners complex in New Mexico causes air pollution in Mesa Verde, Zion and Bryce Canyon National Parks; Everglades National Park in Florida is affected by a Florida Power and Light plant nearby.
- Secretary Watt tried to reverse a decision by former Secretary Cecil Andrus barring stripmining within 5 miles of Yovimpa Point, the most spectacular vista in Bryce Canyon National Park in Utah. Secretary Watt wanted to permit stripmining within view of the park. A federal district court in Utah refused to remand the case to Watt for review.
- Watt has reversed a Park Service decision to phase out motorized rafts operated by private concessioners in the Grand Canyon.
- Watt has supported proposals by snowmobile, off-road vehicle, and airboat organizations to open up certain national park and seashore areas to their uses. Watt has opened Lassen Volcanic National Park in California to snowmobile use; and the Park Service has decided to continue to allow snowmobile use in the Potholes region of Grand Teton National Park, despite a recommendation to the contrary by a blue ribbon panel.

Wilderness

Since the Wilderness Preservation System was created in 1964, it has been the policy of every Administration to protect wilderness from energy and minerals development. The Reagan Administration policy is to open the system to oil, gas, and mineral development, and close off major additions of new lands.

Preamble

Congress created the National Wilderness Preservation System in 1964 "to secure for the American people of present and future generations the benefits of an enduring resource of wilderness." In the terms of the Wilderness Act, "wilderness, in contrast with those areas where man and his own works dominate the landscape, is hereby recognized as an area where the earth and its community of life are untrammeled by man, where man himself is a visitor who does not remain."

The Wilderness System constitutes about 3 percent of the land base of the United States. It includes 23.4 million acres in the lower 48 states and 56.4 million acres in Alaska. All of the wilderness areas are within the federal public lands—in the National Forests, Parks, and Wildlife Refuges, and in the lands managed by the Bureau of Land Management (BLM).

From 1977 to 1979, the Forest Service reviewed 62 million acres of large roadless areas in the National Forests to determine what lands should be recommended to Congress for addition to the wilderness system and what lands should be made available for other uses. When that long study process was complete, the Carter Administration recommended that Congress designate a total of 15 million acres as wilderness. BLM is presently reviewing approximately 24 million acres to determine which lands under its jurisdiction should be recommended to Congress for wilderness designation.

The Wilderness Act allows prospecting and other activities in wilderness areas to collect information about mineral or other resources and requires the Department of the Interior to conduct periodic surveys to determine resource values. In addition, the Wilderness Act allows, but does not require, the Secretary of the Interior to issue energy and mineral leases in wilderness areas until December 31, 1983.

Recognizing that wilderness areas serve vital ecological functions, that they are the last remnants of America's primeval splendor, that they do not contain relatively large amounts of minerals or energy resources, and that they are irreplaceable, every Secretary of the Interior up to the present has, as a matter of policy, opposed mineral or energy development in designated wilderness areas.

Under the Wilderness Act, lands approved for inclusion in the wilderness system will be closed, except for valid existing claims and leases, to mineral and energy development after December 31, 1983.

Charges

Opening Wilderness to Development.

- In May 1981 Secretary Watt directed his Solicitor to find a way to "open wilderness areas." That directive repudiated the policy of every Secretary of the Interior since the Wilderness Act was passed in 1964.
- Secretary Watt advocated a 20–year delay, until 2003, of the date when wilderness lands will be closed to energy and minerals development. Secretary Watt misleadingly stated that delay of the deadline was necessary to inventory oil and gas and other mineral resources. In fact, the Wilderness Act allows, indeed requires, exploration and inventory without any time limit.
- The Forest Service issued draft recommendations to issue leases in the Washakie Wilderness adjacent to Yellowstone National Park, the Ventana Wilderness on California's Big Sur coast, and the Caney Creek Wilderness in Arkansas.
- The Forest Service considered a proposal for seismic exploration in its Bob Marshall Wilderness in Montana. In response, in May 1981, the House Interior Committee directed Secretary Watt to withdraw this area from minerals leasing.
- In November 1981 the Interior Department actually issued a lease for slant drilling into the National Forest's Capitan Wilderness in New Mexico. In recommending this lease, the Forest Service failed to comply with the requirements of law for public notice, public comment, or environmental impact studies.

Expressing alarm at Secretary Watt's actions and advocacy to open up wilderness, the House Interior Committee voted in November 1981 for a six-month moratorium on leasing in wilderness areas.

Faced with firm Congressional opposition, the Administration tried different tactics. In January 1982, Secretary Watt extended the Congressional moratorium on leasing in wilderness until after the current session of Congress and the 1982 elections. Then, in February 1982 Secretary Watt announced a new program, billed as "protection" of wilderness, which actually pursues the same policy of opening wilderness, but under a new guise. He presented the Administration's proposed Wilderness Protection Act of 1982, which would

- Allow the President, without Congressional approval, to open any wilderness area by declaring an undefined "urgent national need." Under the present law, lands designated by Congress as wilderness remain closed to development after December 31, 1983 forever, unless Congress determines otherwise.
- Automatically end protection for the entire wilderness system, opening all wilderness areas to mineral and energy development in the year 2000.

Shutting Off Additions to the Wilderness System.
The Administration wants not only to open the whole wilderness system to energy and mineral development in 2000 but to make sure that, in the meantime, little if any new land is added to the system. The Administration's bill would

- Set short, rigid deadlines for Congress to act on Forest Service and BLM lands recommended for wilderness designation, or recommended for study for designation.
- Give no second chances. Lands not actually designated as wilderness by the deadlines would be permanently released for development. The Forest Service would be barred from ever again studying its lands for wilderness or managing those lands as wilderness, without Congressional approval. Under existing law, wilderness values must be considered in the ongoing, periodic forest planning process.
- Take away from Congress and give to the President the power to determine which BLM wilderness study areas should be released to development. All BLM wilderness study areas would be subject to immediate development.

In addition to its anti-wilderness legislation, the Reagan Administration has, by executive action, attempted to block or limit additions to the Wilderness System.

- Assistant Secretary of Agriculture John Crowell eliminated almost 1 million acres from the previous administration's recommendation to Congress for addition of Forest Service land to the wilderness system.
- Assistant Secretary Crowell has testified against designation of lands recommended for wilderness in the Cranberry area of the Monongahela National Forest, West Virginia; the Big Gump Swamp in the Osceola National Forest, Florida; and Cougar Lakes in the Wenatchee National Forest, Washington.

Fish and Wildlife

In the Reagan Administration, protection of fish and wildlife takes second place to resource development. Secretary Watt has weakened protection of endangered species, downgraded wildlife protection in his crash energy program, sacrificed wildlife for grazing interests, and refused to acquire wildlife habitat authorized by Congress.

Preamble

The federal government is steward of much of the nation's wildlife. Federal wildlife refuges cover over 89 million acres of our public lands. In addition, half a billion acres of publicly owned lands (in National Forests and public lands managed by BLM) are required by law to be managed for multiple uses, one of which is conservation of fish and wildlife.

In addition, several federal laws protect wildlife habitat in state, local, or private ownership against destruction brought about by federal government activities such as dam building and construction of sewers and water treatment plants.

Charges

The Reagan Administration does not have an explicit program for weakening protection of wildlife. Indeed, Secretary of the Interior James Watt lays claim to good stewardship of the nation's wildlife refuges and habitat. The claims are misleading. In fact, under the present Administration, when wildlife and resource development are in conflict, wildlife loses. With few exceptions, whatever gains have been made in wildlife protection during the Reagan Administration were forced on it by Congress, or were a legacy from the past.

Weakening Protection of Endangered Species. The Reagan Administration has

- Paralyzed listing of endangered species. In 14 months the Administration listed only one of the more than two dozen species which had been proposed for listing when President Reagan took office. Listing of that one species (the Hays Spring Amphipod, a tiny invertebrate) has no economic effect whatever, since its only habitat is the Washington Zoo.
- Refused, until threatened with a lawsuit, to list four species that had been finalized by President Carter.
- Bottled up 70 additional listings.
- Proposed cutting 34 percent ($7.9 million) in FY 1982 from the endangered species program, which was already charged with more responsibilities than it could handle on a limited budget. Congress allowed a cut of 24 percent. Secretary Watt has proposed a further cut of $1.2 million for FY 1983.
- Proposed cutting the program for recovery of endangered species in FY 1982. Congress blocked that proposal. The Administration is now claiming credit for completing recovery plans.
- Proposed to reduce endangered species law enforcement staff by 15 positions out of 203, despite increased killing of bald eagles and a large trade in protected species.
- Eliminated $3.9 million in federal funding for state programs to conserve endangered species habitat.

Sacrificing Wildlife Protection for Energy and Grazing Interests. The Reagan Administration has

- Accelerated plans for oil and gas exploration in wildlife refuges in Alaska while proposing a 50 percent cut (from $8 million to less than $4 million) in the Alaska Refuge Management Budget for FY 1982.
- Withdrawn final regulations under the Fish and Wildlife Coordination Act that would have elevated the importance of wildlife habitat values in considering federal permits and federally funded projects.

- Systematically cut funding for vegetation inventories, habitat evaluation, instream flow studies, environmental analyses, and other programs to determine the carrying capacity of public lands to support fish and wildlife and to determine the compatibility between energy development and fish and wildlife protection. At the same time, the Administration has added funds for energy development—thereby increasing the need for the studies being cut.
- Put all of BLM's resources for improvement of the public range into areas where ranchers will get first call for red meat production, leaving little for wildlife.

President Reagan personally

- Rescinded a ten-year-old Executive Order issued by President Nixon that banned the use on the public lands of 1080, a highly toxic poison used to kill coyotes and other predators.

EPA had cancelled registration of 1080 as a predicide and severely limited it use as a rodenticide ten years ago because it poisons nontarget species such as raccoons, badgers, and eagles as well as coyotes. Under the Reagan Administration

- EPA has begun proceedings to re-examine the 1080 ban. EPA Administrator Gorsuch stated that "new information" justified re-opening the issue. A University of California scientist, whose work was cited as the major source of the "new information" has charged that EPA and Gorsuch distorted his findings. "EPA needed some pivotal scientific basis to justify and trigger these hearings," said a spokesman for the University, "so they. . .misrepresented [the scientist's] statements to justify the hearings."
- The Fish and Wildlife Service applied to EPA to approve 1080 for some uses as a predator poison.

Blocking Acquisition of Refuges. Watt claims credit for acquisition of land for several federal and state refuges, all of which he opposed until he was overruled by Congress. Specifically, the Administration has

- Proposed zero funding from the Land and Water Conservation Fund for wildlife refuge acquisition in FY 1982 and only $1.6 million in FY 1983 for partial acquisition of endangered species habitat. At least $54 million is needed from the Fund for buying priority areas, already authorized by Congress for acquisition, to protect them from development and habitat destruction. The two new refuges for which purchase has begun (Bogue Chilto, Louisiana, and Bon Secour, Alabama) were ordered by Congress over Watt's objections.
- Opposed acquisition of privately owned enclaves in refuges in New Jersey, California, and Maine. Congress overruled him.
- Eliminated grants from the Land and Water Conservation Fund for state habitat acquisition.
- Proposed zero funding for wetlands acquisition under the Wetlands Loan Act in FY 1983.

In 1977 the Fish and Wildlife Service identified 1,947,000 acres of wetlands in need of protection under its 10–year duck stamp program.

- The Fish and Wildlife Service purchased only 24,349 acres of wetland—paid for by duck stamps—in the first year of the Reagan Administration. At the Reagan rate of acquisition, it would take 78 years to complete the program. Meanwhile, the nation is losing 600,000 acres of wetland to development every year.
- Watt proposed no new funding for wetlands acquisition under the Wetlands Loan Act in FY 1983. Authority to acquire wetlands under this program expires at the end of FY 1983.

The Administration has announced that it actually intends to divest the National Wildlife Refuge System of a key refuge area. It proposes to

- Transfer National Wildlife Refuge Lands on Matagorda Island to Texas, which wants to use the land for recreation. That use is incompatible with the conservation objectives and special qualities of Matagorda, which provides critical habitat for the highly endangered whooping crane and habitat for several other endangered species.

Cutting Cooperation with States. The Reagan Administration wants to eliminate all federal funding for the Cooperative Wildlife and Fisheries Units. In this program, the Fish and Wildlife Service cooperates with land grant universities and state wildlife agencies in wildlife and fishery research and training. The program trains four out of five of the country's wildlife biologists. Federal funds pay for about one-third of the costs. The Reagan Administration has

- Proposed to cut funding to zero, in both FY 1982 and FY 1983, for the Cooperative Units. Congress restored $4.4 million for the program in FY 1982.

One positive accomplishment of this Administration is the speedup of the ecological mapping inventory of fish and wildlife resources of the Pacific Coast and a start on mapping of the Gulf Coast.

This solitary accomplishment must be judged against the record, outlined above, of relegating fish and wildlife protection to secondary importance.

Energy Leasing

The people of the United States own vast coal, oil shale, oil, and gas resources. These are resources that belonged to the nation when it was founded or were acquired by treaty or by purchase from other nations.

For many decades the nation's energy resources, like other public resources, were made available for private use essentially on demand. Payments to the public treasury were shockingly low, and enormous reserves were leased—not to be developed, but for speculation.

A dozen years ago, President Nixon imposed a moratorium on coal leasing to reassess the way in which leasing decisions were made. In the years that followed, Congress enacted a series of laws requiring the Department of the Interior to consider the interests of the nation as a whole in making energy leasing decisions. The law requires the Department to adhere to five principles. It must

1. Balance potential energy development against alternative uses for the same property, selecting that use that maximizes the benefit to the public.
2. Assure a fair return to the nation for private development of its energy resources.
3. Make resources available only for necessary development, not for speculation.
4. Permit development only where it will not cause irreparable harm to the environment.
5. Provide full and fair opportunities for the public to participate in the decision on how to use the nation's resources.

The Reagan Administration has acted to subvert each of these principles. It seeks to make energy resources available on demand once again. It has truncated the planning process, ignored agricultural, wilderness, environmental, and recreational values, and has excluded the public and state and local governments from the process.

Coal Leasing

The Administration has subverted the leasing system, handing over basic decisions to industry and denigrating the importance of agricultural, environmental, and social and cultural values.

Preamble

There are 16.5 billion tons of federal coal under lease, enough to last over 200 years at the present rate of production of coal from federal leases. In all, the United States owns over 400 billion tons of coal, almost all of it in the West.

Until 1971, coal leasing on federal lands was virtually unregulated. The federal government leased the public lands at giveaway prices. Specula-

tion in coal leases was rampant. Leases were resold at many times the price the government received from the original lease holder. Industry selected the land it wanted to lease and then held the leases idle without producing coal. There was little concern with the public receiving a fair price for leases, with protection of the agricultural or environmental resources, or with the impact of leasing on state and local governments.

President Nixon imposed a moratorium on coal leasing in 1971. And in 1976 Congress sought to end coal leasing abuses with passage of the Federal Coal Leasing Act Amendments, requiring the Interior Department to obtain fair value for the public's coal, to prevent speculation, and to balance coal against other resource values before deciding which tracts to lease.

The Carter Administration put in place a leasing program that met those requirements and proposed to lease federal coal as needed to meet demand for coal production.

Charges

Transferring Control to Industry. The Reagan Administration has abandoned the reforms mandated by the Congress and implemented by the previous administration, and proposes to return to the policies of the past. The Administration has proposed to change the coal leasing regulations to

- Permit industry to make the intial selection of tracts for leasing instead of determining which tracts it is in the public interest to lease, based upon a consideration of alternative uses and environmental values.
- Eliminate independent federal analysis of the level of leasing necessary to meet demand, relying instead on industry to decide how much coal it wants. Leasing in 1981 was up 420 percent from 1980, although the Congressional Office of Technology Assessment recently concluded no new leasing was necessary to meet demand.
- Effectively eliminate restraints on speculation in federal coal by weakening regulations requiring leaseholders to begin production within ten years after obtaining a lease.
- Make consideration of potential economic, social, and environmental effects of coal leasing on a region entirely discretionary.
- Sharply curtail opportunities for participation by the public and by state and local governments in leasing decisions and reduce the amount of information available to the public about leasing.
- Eliminate requirements that lease applicants submit information to the U.S. Attorney General for antitrust review.

Cutting Back Planning and Environmental Analysis. Since coming to office the Administration has not only massively increased leasing, but at the same time has significantly reduced the funds and personnel for environmental planning and management.

The result is that the Department of the Interior is simply unable to assess or consider the value of any other use than coal development for tracts requested by industry.

Outer Continental Shelf Oil Leasing

The Reagan Administration has proposed changes in the program for offshore oil and gas leasing which will have devastating impacts on our coasts, on state planning functions, on public participation, and, ironically, on our ability to inventory and develop our offshore resources. These new policies will deprive the public of a fair return for the sale of public oil and gas and will ultimately delay their development.

Preamble

The United States owns over 1 billion acres of offshore submerged lands on the Outer Continental Shelf (OCS). Since the Outer Continental Shelf Lands Act was enacted in 1953, the Department has leased approximately 27 million acres for oil and gas development, resulting in 8,000 producing wells yielding 5 billion barrels of oil and 44 trillion cubic feet of gas. Offshore waters currently produce about 9 percent of our nation's oil and 20 percent of our domestic gas. In 1980, the Carter Administration proposed to double the amount of leased acreage by 1986.

Charges

Accepting Low Royalties and Allowing Speculation. The Administration has proposed

- Leasing every year nearly ten times as many acres offshore as have been leased in the entire 29–year history of the leasing program.
- Allowing only 2 years between sales in frontier (not previously leased) areas, despite the fact that most coastal states have argued repeatedly that they need 3 years to deal with the impacts of each new lease sale in these undeveloped areas.
- Elimination of both tract-specific geohazard analysis and tract specific geologic analysis (estimating the amount of oil and gas which underlies a particular tract). This Administration has often touted the importance of knowing the costs and benefits of an action. Yet they propose to eliminate two of the most important factors in any cost-benefit analysis: the value of the resource, and the potential risk from geohazards.
- Repeal of the Failure and Inventory System (FIRS), which the National Academy of Sciences in a recent report said should be strengthened.
- Elimination of the requirement that detailed development and production plans be filed in the western

Gulf of Mexico and the Santa Barbara Channel, even though they are required elsewhere.
- Changing the regulations which required an exploration plan to be filed at the end of the second year of a five-year lease. The exploration plan will not be required until the end of the fourth year of a five year lease, thus reducing the incentives for leaseholders to diligently develop the resource.
- Lowering the royalty rate on many offshore areas from 16–2/3 percent to 12–1/2 percent. Is this the way to balance the budget?

Disregarding Public Concerns. Accelerated OCS oil and gas development threatens habitat, offshore and onshore. Problems include disposal of drilling muds, construction of onshore support facilities, operational as well as catastrophic oil spills, and aesthetic impacts. Damage to local economies dependent on tourism and commercial fisheries is of significant concern to Governors of several states.

The Administration has proposed

- Repeal of the regulation which requires public notification of the filing of an offshore development and production plan.
- Zero funding for coastal zone management grants to states—the only mechanism which encourages state planning for the impacts of offshore and coastal development.

Several states have sued the Administration when their views were not taken into account. The Commerce Department issued and then was forced by public opposition to withdraw regulations that would have prevented states from having any meaningful role in OCS planning.

Oil Shale Leasing

The Administration seeks to accelerate private acquisition of publicly owned shale reserves, when neither the economic nor the environmental consequences of shale development are known.

Preamble

About 80 percent of the nation's 400 million barrels of recoverable shale oil, most of it in Colorado and Utah, is on federal public lands. Shale development enjoyed a brief boom and then suffered a quick bust more than half a century ago. Shale oil was then and remains now more expensive to produce than oil.

In 1974 the United States leased four shale tracts in Colorado and Utah to a consortium of oil companies at a 2 percent royalty plus a bonus of 8.5 cents per recoverable barrel of oil. The price of oil was then about $8 per barrel. A variety of government agencies have poured research and development money into shale projects over the past half century.

Water Resources

The Reagan Administration recently gave several billion dollars in loan and price guarantees to two oil company shale projects in Colorado.

Shale development is surrounded by uncertainties both economic and environmental. There are no commercial size shale operations in the United States and no one can say with certainty whether shale oil can be produced at a price competitive with crude oil. Nor has industry yet shown that it can safely dispose of the vast quantities of waste generated by shale production. These uncertainties led Interior Secretary Morton to conclude in 1974 that further leasing should await data from the development of tracts already under lease.

Charges

Leasing at High Risk and Low Gain for the Public. The Administration has put aside caution and supports legislation that would

- Increase the number of leases and the amount of land that could be held by a single company. This will permit concentration of control of our shale resources among a few companies.
- Fail to provide any guarantee that leased shale would be developed. Industry will be permitted to hold leases for speculation and resell them at inflated prices.
- Ignore the need for environmental and socioeconomic planning.
- Establish no guarantee that the public will receive a fair price from the private developers of its shale resources.

Secretary Watt has ordered BLM to write shale leasing regulations to

- Permit leasing on industry demand without consideration of the need for leasing and with little analysis of the impact of shale development on water resources, local communities, or wildlife.
- Allow leasing without requiring diligent development of leased resources, or securing a fair economic return for the public.

The Reagan Administration has done little to take the fat out of pork barrel water projects. Its approach is politics as usual. The President proposes spending at near-record levels for water projects, including projects that are indefensibly wasteful and damaging to the environment.

Preamble

Water resource projects—building dams and channels, dredging ports, opening water ways—are of course an old and legitimate activity of the federal government. They have earned the name of "pork barrel" because they so often involve waste and subsidies. They frequently do serious environmental damage.

The "cost-benefit" analyses of the U.S. Army Corps of Engineers and the Interior Department's Bureau of Reclamation (the two big water project agencies) are a longtime scandal. These agencies include in their calculations questionable benefits and projections based on interest rates as low as 3 1/4 percent.

For example, court documents on the Tennessee-Tombigbee Waterway (the biggest water project in the nation's history) show that the Corps of Engineers disguised the project's real cost because it would have had too great an "emotional" impact on Congress. Other documents show that the Corps claimed benefits for companies which had stated categorically they would not use the canal, and for other companies that no longer existed.

The Bureau of Reclamation, which operates entirely in the West, has no better record. Some of the Bureau's biggest projects involve huge subsidies to a few users. For example, in the Central Arizona project, Federal taxpayers will be spending about $1.8 million for every farm using the Project's water for irrigation.

The following table shows that on the average irrigators served by the Bureau are paying back less than 10 percent of the costs underwritten by taxpayers—and with no interest.

Project	Investment per Acre	Repaid by Irrigator
Garrison Diversion (ND)	$3753	$ 77
Dolores (CO)	4301	209
O'Neill Unit (NE)	4535	588
North Loup (NE)	4678	515
Central Utah Project (Bonneville Unit)	1825	68
Central Arizona Project	1274	59

Citizens worked hard with the last Administration to bring some sense to water project planning. Rational economic standards were developed for the Corps and the Bureau to use in assessing projects, and conservation requirements were included in contracts to supply water to communities from Corps and Bureau reservoirs. These steps were just a beginning in the tough job of getting pork barrel projects under control.

Charges

The Reagan Administration despite its rhetoric on ending waste in government has abandoned tough economic analysis for water projects.

Supporting Pork Barrel Spending. The Reagan Administration has

● Recommended spending $3.8 billion in FY 1983 for water projects—nearly the highest ever—and a 23 percent increase for Bureau of Reclamation spending. All of the Bureau's projects are in the West, where environmental problems from dam building and water diversions are often acute.

The Administration has greatly increased funding for some of the Bureau's worst, most wasteful and damaging projects. For example

● The Administration proposes to spend an additional $1.2 billion for the white elephant Bonneville Unit of the Central Utah Project—which was listed as 22 percent complete in 1980, with remaining costs to complete of $584 million. It is now shown as only 18 percent complete with over $1 billion to go for completion, because of staggering cost overruns and soaring prices. This project will take 136,000 acre feet of fresh water out of the Colorado River Basin, aggravating salinity problems downstream. By dumping additional water in Salt Lake, it will aggravate the lake's rising water level, which is endangering shoreline recreation and industries and the airport. It will take away from the Ute Indians water which will have to be replaced, at a cost not figured into the project's cost estimate. And it will adversely affect 200 miles of fishing streams, destroy 28,000 miles of waterfront habitat, and reduce the warm water fishery in Lake Utah by one-third. As with many other costly damaging projects, there are alternatives to this project; Salt Lake County has proposed a list of seven.

Two steps taken by the Reagan Administration are worthy of real commendation. One is its proposal for a users' fee for deepdraft harbors and inland waterways, thus ending much of the subsidy to the commercial craft which use these waterways.

The other is a proposed cut in the Soil Conservation Services' small watershed program. This program has dammed and channelized hundreds of small streams over the past 25 years, with little effect on floods and less regard for soil erosion and other environmental damage.

Dropping Requirements for Economic Justification, Conservation, and Public Participation. The Reagan Administration has

● Eliminated the recently developed principles for economic justification of water projects, on the grounds that they constitute a "burden." Ironically, the "burden" is not on the private sector, but on the Corps and the Bureau, to bring their performance up to private enterprise standards.
● Struck down the conservation requirements for communities supplied by the Corps and the Bureau reservoirs.
● Reduced public participation in Bureau water delivery contracts. This means that big landowners, who have been able to get lucrative deals with the Bureau in the past when no one was watching could do so again. The potential loss to the Treasury is hundreds of millions of dollars.

Dismantling the Wetlands Protection Program. The Reagan Administration has also begun to dismantle the wetlands protection under Section 404 of the Clean Water Act.

● The Army Corps, with the concurrence of EPA, proposes to reduce the jurisdiction of the program so drastically that 85 percent of the nation's wetlands would no longer be protected under the 404 program.

Energy

In one year the Reagan Administration has turned federal energy policy to chaos. Reagan officials have used free market rhetoric as a sword against programs they dislike: energy conservation, solar energy, emergency preparedness. But they have sheathed the sword with respect to nuclear power, synthetic fuels, and the oil industry.

The Administration wants to eliminate almost every program that provides assistance, information, or protection to energy consumers, while leaving intact a $16 billion synthetic fuels subsidy program, tax breaks worth several billion dollars a year to the oil industry, and direct subsidies to the nuclear industry of at least $1 billion a year.

Reagan officials speak boldly of massive increases in production of energy, while the nation's and the world's energy producers cut back in the face of energy conservation's quiet revolution.

Most alarmingly, the Administration has sought to weaken environmental, safety, and health regulations in every area that relates to energy, from nuclear reactor safety to power plant air pollution. It has done so in the face of increasing evidence that those governmental protections are critical to our safety, our health, and the quality of our environment.

Nuclear Power

The free market is killing nuclear power. Instead of letting it fend for itself, President Reagan wants to rescue the industry with continued heavy subsidies, watered down safety regulations, and reduced safeguards against the spread of nuclear weapons.

Preamble

Since the Reagan Administration took office, six nuclear power plants already under construction have been cancelled. The Nuclear Regulatory Commission staff predicts nineteen more cancellations in the near future of plants under construction. Although the cancellations involve billions of dollars in losses, the utilities involved concluded that completion of the plants would cause far greater financial losses. More proposed reactors have been cancelled during the past ten years than are now operating in the United States.

The nuclear industry has also been plagued by safety problems and mismanagement. The accidents at Brown's Ferry and Three Mile Island exposed serious flaws in reactor safety systems. Middle-aged plants are now suffering unexpected breakdowns. The recent accident at Ginna, New York, where a ruptured pipe released radioactive gas, was the fourth such incident in recent years. The Nuclear

Regulatory Commission suspended the operating license of the controversial Diablo Canyon plant only days after it was granted because critical parts of the reactor's earthquake protection system were built backwards. A Nuclear Regulatory Commission investigation found many more design errors that affect safety.

The abiding problems of nuclear weapons proliferation and waste disposal were a serious concern to both the Ford and Carter Administrations. President Ford deferred commercial reprocessing of spent nuclear fuel pending an assessment of international safeguards against proliferation. President Carter deferred commercial reprocessing and tabled development of the plutonium breeder reactor because of dangers of proliferation.

Charges

President Reagan has abandoned his predecessors' caution on nuclear power. Contrary to his own free market philosophy, he has spared nuclear power from the budget axe. Ignoring the industry's real financial, management, and technical problems, he blames the industry's plight on "overregulation," and has moved to weaken safety regulations and safeguards against proliferation.

Maintaining Subsidies. The Reagan budget for FY 1983 would maintain direct subsidies to the nuclear power industry at a level of more than $1 billion per year—added to estimated subsidies of at least $37 billion which the taxpayers have already sunk in the industry.

The Reagan budget would

- Commit more than twice as much energy research and development money to the Liquid Metal Fast Breeder Reactor (LMFBR) as to *all* other forms of energy (coal, shale, solar, conservation), despite the fact that the LMFBR is outmoded and uneconomic.
- Pour $253 million into the Clinch River Breeder Reactor, a demonstration LMFBR for which total projected costs have skyrocketed from $700 million to $3.5 billion. Taxpayers would be stuck with 90 percent of the bill, although industry had originally agreed to pay half.

The Carter Administration's position was to close out the Clinch River project while pursuing basic research. All the available facts on costs show it is folly to put hundreds of million of the taxpayers' dollars into the Clinch River project. For example, France dropped plans to build five more LMFBRs after paying the bill for the first one, which cost twice as much as a comparable light water reactor.

Dropping Barriers to Proliferation. The Clinch River Breeder Reactor is not only hugely wasteful; its use of plutonium for fuel creates dangers of proliferation of nuclear weapons. So does the commercial reprocessing of spent nuclear powerplant fuel which the Reagan Administration is supporting. Even worse is the proposal, now under active consideration, to use plutonium recovered from commercial powerplant fuel for a greatly accelerated program of making bombs for the U.S. military.

- President Reagan has lifted the Ford-Carter ban on private reprocessing of nuclear fuel and the Administration is now actively promoting such private ventures in the United States.
- The Reagan Administration has reversed a decade-long policy of slowing the spread of sensitive nuclear technologies, and is considering the export of classified technology for enriching uranium. It has also lifted the ban on supplying military and economic aid to Pakistan, a country known to be developing nuclear weapons, without any new guarantees of Pakistan's future direction in this sensitive area.
- The Department of Energy is developing an advanced enrichment technology which would make it possible to obtain weapons grade plutonium from commercial spent fuel, and is actively considering proposals to "mine" commercial spent fuel pools for bomb material. Such a course of action would effectively destroy the distinction between the civilian and military uses of nuclear power, ending forever the "Atoms for Peace" idea and making nuclear non-proliferation a clear impossiblity.

Weakening Safety Protection. The Administration, in echoing the industry's complaints about overregulation, is ignoring real safety problems which can be controlled only by effective government regulation. The Administration is also pushing ahead with nuclear waste disposal plans, without adequate scientific knowledge and technical preparation.

- The Nuclear Regulatory Commission has shifted resources away from safety issues into an accelerated licensing program.
- The Department of Energy has dumped the comprehensive, conservative, safety-oriented nuclear waste policy developed by a broad interagency group under the Carter Administration. Stating that the major technical problems have been solved, the Reagan Administration is rushing ahead with waste burial plans. It is de-emphasizing the rights of states and localities to adequate information and a voice in siting.

Energy Conservation

Energy conservation is the cheapest, quickest and cleanest way to meet the nation's energy needs. The Administration has sought to abolish, dismantle, or destroy almost every Federal program that promotes conservation.

Preamble

The United States now spends more than $385 billion a year on energy. The bill would be far larger if we had not made improvements over the last decade in the efficiency with which we use energy. Almost 90 percent of the growth in the U.S. economy between 1973 and 1980 was made possible by energy conservation (the economy grew 19 percent in real terms, energy consumption only grew 2 percent.)

Energy from new sources costs more than energy from old sources because it costs more to build a powerplant or find new oil than it used to. Thus, the only way to reduce the cost of energy to the nation is to reduce the amount we consume by using energy more efficiently. Indeed, the temporary oil "glut" that has lowered world oil prices is partly due to reduced demand resulting from energy conservation.

For low and moderate income families, the issue may be survival as heating costs consume up to half of their income. The only way they can reduce their costs other than freezing is by insulating, caulking, and adding storm windows so as to use less energy and less money to keep warm.

The Oak Ridge National Laboratory estimates that federal conservation programs saved the United States $12 billion during 1980 alone. The Administration's own estimates put the 1980 savings at $3.4 billion. And once in place, conservation measures continue to yield savings year after year.

Charges

Cutting the Conservation Budget. The Administration has sought to eliminate virtually every federal energy conservation program. It has proposed to reduce the budget for conservation by 97 percent. That would

- Halt federal research on conservation that has already yielded innovations that have saved many times the cost of the program.
- Eliminate most state energy conservation offices.
- Eliminate federal assistance for the weatherization of schools and hospitals.
- Halt the flow of technical information to consumers, businesses and local governments on the means to improve energy efficiency.

Eliminating Assistance for Individuals. The Administration has

- Tried to abolish the Solar and Conservation Bank, despite the intent of Congress. Congress passed legislation creating the Bank in 1980 to provide low interest financing for solar and conservation measures. The Administration proposed to eliminate it. When Congress said "no," the Administration simply refused to obey the law and did nothing to set up the Bank.
- Sought to eliminate the conservation tax credit while expanding tax benefits for energy producers.

- Proposed to eliminate the low income weatherization program. Under this program, the federal government directly assists low income people to invest in caulking and insulating their homes. This investment could remove the need for continuing government assistance to people unable to pay huge heating bills.

Dismantling Regulatory Programs Designed to Help Consumers. The Administration has

- Refused to obey the law that requires it to issue efficiency standards for furnaces, refrigerators, and other appliances. American appliances, as American automobiles did, are falling far behind their Japanese competitors. Efficiency improvements would save literally billions of dollars as well as energy.
- Sought to abolish the Residential Conservation Services Program that provides low cost home energy audits to consumers.
- Abandoned stricter fuel efficiency standards for automobiles after 1985.

Conservation is the energy program that puts money back in the pockets of individual American citizens. The Administration regards it with contempt.

Solar Energy

Government support for solar energy is in eclipse. While opinion polls show the public favors solar energy over all the alternatives, President Reagan has done his best to end federal support for renewable energy. If solar energy ultimately prospers, it will be in spite of federal policy.

Preamble

The public has good reasons for supporting solar energy. It is clean, infinitely renewable, and cannot be embargoed or dominated by a cartel. The use of solar energy does not pollute the air, poison our waters, or produce material for nuclear weapons. The production of renewable energy equipment creates more jobs and distributes them more fairly than the search for oil and gas, and the money stays in the United States.

Because of these special qualities, President Carter set a goal of meeting 20 percent of all our energy needs from renewable sources by the year 2000. Repeated studies, including one by the Harvard Business School and another by the Solar Energy Research Institute, have documented that this goal could be met at a lower cost than getting the same amount of energy from traditional sources.

However, numerous obstacles hinder the achievement of this goal. Solar energy systems often cost more to buy; the savings accrue over time with the reduction or elimination of fuel bills. The higher first cost is particularly troublesome during periods of

high interest rates. The price of fossil fuels and nuclear energy remains artificially low due to the effect of past and continuing subsidies. Consumers and businesses need to be assured that the new technologies will work as well as the old. Some solar technologies, particularly photovoltaic cells and biomass systems, require more research and mass production to reduce costs. All of these problems were the subject of government efforts initiated by the Ford and Carter Administrations.

Charges

In little more than a year, the federal solar energy program has been reduced to shambles.

Heading the Solar Budget Toward Zero. The Reagan Administration has cut the solar budget by 87 percent and will seek to eliminate the solar program. The Administration has already

- Slashed federally supported research at the very time when other countries, notably Germany, France, and Japan, are stepping up their support for solar research. Thus, the United States is likely to lose world markets.
- Stopped the flow of information on solar systems to consumers. Millions of consumers have received practical and reliable information on solar from the government in the past.
- Fired the Director and 300 staff members of the Solar Energy Research Institute, (SERI) the world's premier solar laboratory.
- Suppressed a SERI study showing the potential of solar and conservation measures and reporting on public opinion surveys that show popular support for renewable energy development.

The Administration has abandoned efforts to stimulate growth of a photovoltaics industry (using sunlight to make electricity directly), dropping efforts to use photovoltaics in government installations.

There are few solar regulations. However, the few that exist have not been overlooked in the Administration's war on solar energy.

Eliminating Assistance to Consumers. The Administration has sought to cut the programs that would provide direct aid to consumers. It has

- Fired the staff, stopped the regulations, and asked Congress to abolish the Solar and Conservation Bank, which would provide low-interest financing for individuals installing solar devices and for builders. When Congress twice refused to abolish the bank, the Administration simply defied the law and did nothing to set up the bank.
- Proposed to eliminate the tax credit for persons installing solar equipment. This average citizens' energy tax loophole was to be closed, while the oil industry's loopholes were enlarged. Congress rejected the proposal. The Administration is trying again to abolish this credit for businesses (not for residences).

- Asked Congress to eliminate the Residential Conservation Service Program, which provides homeowners with energy audits for a nominal charge. When Congress refused to do so, the Administration proposed changes in the regulations that would make it extremely difficult to include in the audits an evaluation of the cost-effectiveness of solar energy.
- Proposed to repeal the law that requires utilities to use electricity generated by windmills, very small hydropower projects and industrial co-generators of steam and electricity.

Synthetic Fuels

President Reagan attacked subsidies for synthetic fuels while he was campaigning, but in office he has maintained them. Meanwhile his Administration has essentially halted efforts to develop rules to control pollution from synthetic fuel plants.

Preamble

Coal and oil shale can be converted into liquid and gaseous fuels. The United States has huge reserves of both coal and oil shale. We do not now use them to make liquid and gaseous fuels, because the resulting products would cost much more than the oil and gas available as alternatives.

The Carter Administration proposed and won approval of a multi-billion dollar synthetic fuels subsidy to be adminstered by an autonomous, federally financed Synthetic Fuels Corporation. The Corporation spends public money, but is exempt from the laws that make other federal agencies accountable to the public.

Synthetic fuels production is potentially a source of large quantities of hazardous waste, air, and water pollution. Because we have little experience with synthetic fuels plants, we do not know how effective pollution controls will be.

Ronald Reagan attacked the use of tax funds to subsidize synthetic fuels when he was campaigning, and members of his transition team recommended that he abolish the corporation.

Charges

Continuing Subsidies.

- Instead of abolishing synthetic fuels subsidies, President Reagan personally approved over three billion dollars in loan and price guarantees for three projects in the West, two owned by oil companies.
- He has also refused to cut back on the Synthetic Fuels Corporation. The Corporation will soon begin to award an additional 12 billion dollars in subsidies to other synthetic fuels projects.

Disregarding Environmental Controls. The EPA had initiated intensive efforts to develop a program to assure that the massive synthetic fuels plants built with Federal assistance would use the best possible pollution control technology. Gorsuch terminated that effort. Since she took office EPA has

- Scrapped Pollution Control Guidance documents for synthetic fuels plants that had been developed to provide guidance for plant designers and environmental officials.
- Proposed to virtually eliminate research on the health, safety, and environmental effects of synthetic fuels plants

———————————————

Regulatory Reform

Under the cloak of "reform", the Reagan Administration is carrying out a program to eliminate protection of the public and participation by the public in the formation of environmental policy through regulation.

Preamble

There is little economic incentive for industry to control pollution. The "free market" does nothing to protect wilderness or wildlife. It is only through governmental action that we have reduced pollution, created national parks, controlled the ravages of stripmining and, in general, sought to protect the quality of our lives. Much of what government does is accomplished by setting rules for private behavior. The Congress, in laws enacted to protect human health and the environment, has required federal agencies to make such rules.

Charges

Under the Reagan Administration, "Regulatory Reform" is a euphemism. In practice, it has come to mean reduced opportunities for public participation in policy making, increased opportunities for industry participation in government decisions, delayed action on many rules that are essential to protect the environment, health and safety, and increased emphasis on reducing costs to industry even where the result is increased risk for the public.

Putting Economics Ahead of Health and Safety. Shortly after he came to office, President Reagan issued Executive Order 12291. That order allows the Office of Management and Budget (OMB) to review regulations both before they are proposed and again before they are promulgated, to order review of existing regulations, to delay regulations, and to require increased consideration of industry objections regarding the cost of a regulation. OMB has fulfilled its mandate with enthusiasm and a notable disregard for the human and environmental consequences of its actions. OMB is a budget agency. It has no environmental, safety, or health expertise.

- OMB has exercised its authority over dozens of environmental regulations. The result has been suspension of pre-treatment regulations for industrial effluents, suspension of insurance regulations for hazardous waste handlers, and delay in the labeling of toxic substances in the workplace.
- Deeming itself exempt from the fairness and openness requirements applicable to other agencies, OMB has operated in secret and served as a special conduit for private industry contacts.

Excluding the Public. Throughout the Government, public access to information has been reduced. The Administration has proposed to cut back on the Freedom of Information Act, and agencies have already cut back on information they voluntarily disclose. The pattern is particularly obvious in the environmental area. Congress wrote unique and broadranging public participation requirements into the environmental laws, *because those laws are designed to protect the public.* The Administration seems to regard public participation as an obstacle to smooth relations with industry.

- Secretary Watt has proposed to reduce opportunities for members of the public to participate in decisions on leasing, land use, strip mining, and wilderness.
- EPA Chief of Staff Daniel has recommended a sweeping revision of EPA public participation policies to reduce public access.
- The Agriculture Department has proposed revisions to land management planning regulations for the Forest Service which substantially reduce requirements for public notice and opportunities for public comment in the planning process.
- The Agriculture Department also withheld from the public, and finally released only under pressure, unfavorable comments on its soil conservation program.
- EPA has destroyed hundreds of publications designed to provide information on pollution.
- EPA has imposed severe constraints on the publication by its scientists of research results and scientific data.

The Administration's Regulatory Reform program seems to operate from the assumption that the public has little business interfering with government and that industry should not be required to reduce the level of environmenal pollution, cancer-producing food additives, dangerous and defective products, or workplace hazards unless the public can prove that the *economic* value of health, safety, and environmental protection exceeds their cost to industry.

Council on Environmental Quality

The Council on Environmental Quality was a small, high-level, very effective agency for environmental analysis, reporting, policy coordination, and advice to the President. The Reagan Administration has reduced it to a shell.

Preamble

The Council was formed on January 1, 1970, when President Nixon signed the National Environmental Policy Act (NEPA) into law. As part of the President's "extended family" in his Executive Office, the Council has been active in policy initiatives, interagency coordination, and Presidential advice, according to the desires of the President. Throughout its first eleven years, CEQ fulfilled its duties of implementing NEPA (including overseeing requirements for environmental impact statements), reporting every year on the state of the environment, and commissioning and supervising environmental studies of national significance.

In its first three years, under President Nixon, the Council produced three Presidential Environmental Messages, chaired interagency task forces, and helped to draft major legislation. Again, during the Carter years, the Council was active in policy matters, preparing two Environmental Messages from the President, developing regulations under NEPA, and leading government-wide initiatives on environmental issues. Among the many issues to which the Council brought policy leadership were toxic substances control, ocean pollution, farmland preservation, the effect of government programs on land use, wildlife law, integrated pest management, energy and its environmental effects, acid rain, and interrelated global resource, population and environmental problems.

Throughout its first eleven years, until the close of 1980, the Council was the major source of information and analysis for both government and public use on broad environmental policy matters (as opposed to more technical reports from regulatory agencies like EPA). In addition to its eleven Annual Reports, the Council sponsored or cosponsored such landmark reports as *The Quiet Revolution in Land Use Control* (1971), *Integrated Pest Management* (1972), *The Costs of Sprawl* (1974), *OCS Oil and Gas—An Environmental Assessment* (1975), *The Evolution of Wildlife Law* (1977), *Environmental Saatistics* (1980), *The Global 2000 Report to the President* (1980), *Desertification of the United States* (1981), and *The National Agricultural Lands Study* (1981).

A number of distinguished people served as Members of the Council during its first 11 years. Among them were the first two Chairmen (under the Nixon and Ford Administrations): Russell Train, a lifelong conservation leader and later Administrator of EPA, and Russell Peterson, a former Republican Governor of Delaware and environmental leader.

Charges

The Reagan Administration has

- Cut CEQ's budget from $3.1 million (FY 1980) to $919,000 (FY 1982). This cut of $2 million had no fiscal significance. Rather, it was a policy choice to signal the downgrading of environmental issues in the Reagan White House.
- Dismissed the Council's entire professional staff of 30 people in May 1981. Some of the staff had served since the Nixon and Ford Administrations. No CEQ professional staff member had ever been dismissed in any previous change of administrations. The new professional staff of CEQ numbers about half a dozen.
- Appointed as Chairman of the Council Alan Hill, a California businessman whose previous experience in environmental issues was as a mid-level state official during the Reagan governorship. President Reagan designated as a CEQ Member James MacAvoy, who proved unacceptable to Congress because of his record of strong opposition to federal action on acid rain.

With the drastic reduction in CEQ's funds and the dismissal of all experienced staff, the Council's activities have been effectively stilled.

The International Environment

When the Reagan Administration took office, the United States was a recognized world leader in protecting the international environment. Now we are bringing up the rear. Despite a few bright spots, the overall Reagan record is poor.

Preamble

U.S. concern for protection of the world environment is longstanding, dating at least from the seal and migratory bird treaties early in this century. With the environmental ferment of the early 1970s and the preparations for the 1972 Stockholm Conference on the Human Environment, we stepped into a strong world leadership position.

The Carter Administration undertook a systematic approach to interrelated global resource, population, and environmental problems. Following the appearance in July 1980 of the *Global 2000 Report to the President*, an interagency study recommended a strong, integrated approach and many specific U.S. initiatives to address these problems.

Charges

The Reagan Administration was presented with a unique opportunity for leadership on vital issues affecting the world environment, resources, and population. With only few exceptions, its response has been negative.

Sacrificing Protection of the International Environment in Favor of Business Interests. The Reagan approach in general has been one of boosterism for private business interests, with little regard for dangers to the international environment and public health. The President or his appointees have

- Greatly relaxed U.S. efforts to prevent nuclear weapons proliferation by restricting trade in weapons-usable materials, most notably plutonium. The Administration has returned to a policy of promoting nuclear exports with scant regard to the danger of the spread of nuclear weapons.
- Revoked President Carter's Executive Order controlling U.S. exports of banned products and substances.
- Jeopardized approval by the world community of a Law of the Sea Treaty resulting from more than 10 years of negotiations involving more than 100 nations.

Stalling Action on Urgent Issues. Reagan or his appointed officials have

- Fired the nonpolitical head of the Department of Energy's research program on the effects of carbon dioxide buildup on the earth's climate.
- Stalled vital international negotiations aimed at harmonizing regulation of toxic substances by the Western industrialized nations.
- Reversed the U.S. position favoring increased regulation of trade in certain endangered or rare species (*e.g.*, parrots), signalling abandonment of U.S. leadership in this important area.
- Downgraded international efforts by the National Park Service and the Fish and Wildlife Service, which have historically provided substantial assistance to other nations in natural resource management.
- Proposed cutting to zero the U.S. funding, under the World Heritage Convention, for protection of natural areas of unique importance.
- Proposed to slash the U.S. contribution to the United Nations Environment Programme by 80% in Fiscal Year 1982 and, after the Congress refused to go along, recommended a 70 percent cut for FY 1983.
- Refused to provide any funds for a major program of regional cooperation to stop pollution of the Caribbean. Several European countries, including France and Great Britain, are contributing to the program.
- Threatened to cut drastically U.S. support for international population programs, and relented only under an avalanche of criticism.

The do-nothing attitude of the Administration has sometimes reached the level of absurdity. Recently, for example, the head of EPA's international office made repeated, time-consuming, and highly visible efforts to prevent the public release of an innocuous staff report by an international agency on global resource issues.

The Administration has taken positive steps in a few areas.

The Administration took excellent positions at the July 1981 meeting of the International Whaling Commission.

A number of Federal agencies co-sponsored a November 1981 conference on conserving the earth's biological diversity.

The Administration established in September 1981 a Global Issues Working Group to discuss a coordinated response to population, resource, and environmental issues. However, the Working Group has accomplished little thus far.

The few positive actions have been far outweighed by negative actions and by malign neglect in the form of prolonged delays.

What You Can Do

If you have read this Indictment and are distressed, as we are, at the environmental tragedy unfolding under the Reagan Administration, we urge you to act.

- Ask to meet with your Senators and Congressman when they are home for the Easter or Memorial Day Congressional recess. Suggest that they hold local hearings on the issues raised by the Indictment.
- Talk to local government and press representatives about the local impacts of the Administration's policies.

The environmental laws were passed because the public demanded them. Public support can save them.

A Major Power Failure

March 24, 1982

From a coalition of energy, environmental, scientific,
and consumer groups representing millions of Americans.

Center for
Renewable Resources

The Cousteau Society

Environmental Action

Environmental
Action Foundation

Environmental Defense Fund

F.A.S.

Federation of
American Scientists

Friends of the Earth

National Audubon Society

Natural Resources
Defense Council

The Nuclear Club

NIRS

Nuclear Information
and Resource Service

Sierra Club

Solar Lobby

**UNION OF
CONCERNED
SCIENTISTS**

Union of
Concerned Scientists

THE REAGAN ENERGY PLAN

- -

A MAJOR POWER FAILURE

A Report From

CENTER FOR RENEWABLE RESOURCES
COUSTEAU SOCIETY
ENVIRONMENTAL ACTION
ENVIRONMENTAL ACTION FOUNDATION
ENVIRONMENTAL DEFENSE FUND
FEDERATION OF AMERICAN SCIENTISTS
FRIENDS OF THE EARTH
NATIONAL AUDUBON SOCIETY
NATURAL RESOURCES DEFENSE COUNCIL
THE NUCLEAR CLUB, INC.
NUCLEAR INFORMATION AND RESOURCE SERVICE
SIERRA CLUB
SOLAR LOBBY
UNION OF CONCERNED SCIENTISTS

MARCH 24, 1982
WASHINGTON, D.C.

PREFACE

Unbearably expensive, socially disruptive, and needlessly damaging to the long-term national interest, President Reagan's energy policies represent a major retreat from the progress of the past few years toward a sensible national energy policy. As this report documents, the Administration is ignoring public and expert opinion. It is abandoning programs for increasing energy efficiency and the use of renewable energy resources to meet U.S. energy needs and promoting, instead, energy technologies that are less reliable and more expensive.

During the past year, the Administration has acted irrationally and irresponsibly by cutting federally sponsored conservation and solar programs, disregarding environmental and economic values in the leasing and development of federal energy resources, and proposing increased subsidies to nuclear energy—one of the most costly and dangerous of available energy sources.

We are alarmed that so few Americans are aware of the immediate costs and long-term significance of the Administration's energy proposals. We believe that our energy problems can only deepen and become more intractable if the public does not press Congress and the Administration to back out of ill-advised commitments to nuclear power and to vigorously support more reliable and economic energy sources. This report tells why.

I. INTRODUCTION

In policy statements, budget proposals, and administrative actions the Administration has gradually revealed its vision of what American energy policy should be and where the Nation's energy development efforts should be focused. It has become clear that the Administration believes that the nation's energy problem is one solely of increasing energy supply. In adopting this view the Reagan Administration fails to understand that our needs are not for fuels themselves, but for the services they supply. Warmth, mobility, lighting, goods--these are the desired results, and our national objective ought to be to supply these services as efficiently as possible. Moreover, it is clear that these basic needs can be met in many different ways, some of them far more economic and less risky than others.

Unfortunately, no evidence indicates that the Reagan Administration understands the real nature of the energy problem. Nor that it has attempted to analyze the benefits and costs of alternative approaches to dealing with the challenge. Rather, having made up its mind, the Administration appears determined not to be confused by facts. With uninformed certainty, it is

-Increasing reliance on nuclear fission, encouraging the introduction of a global plutonium economy;

-Accelerating and subsidizing the production of oil, gas, coal, synthetic fuels, and oil shales by sacrificing environmental protection, reducing local participation in leasing decision making, underpricing national energy resources, and providing long-term economic subsidies;

-Drastically truncating federal support for increasing national energy efficiency and the use of renewable energy resources; and

-Cutting back energy-assistance programs for those hardest hit by rising energy prices.

By almost any measure--economic efficiency, national security, impacts on inflation, effects on employment, environmental damage--these proposals amount to putting the worst first. The damaging effects of these decisions will be felt for many years and in many ways.

While the Administration's budget for the Department of Energy (DOE) by no means presents a complete picture of its intentions, it shows clearly enough the Administration's energy priorities. As the figure on the next page shows, DOE funding for solar energy and conservation programs has fallen sharply since 1980. If the Administration's budget proposals for fiscal year 1983 are accepted, conservation programs will be cut by 98 percent from the 1980 level, renewable resources by 86 percent, and fossil fuels by 87 percent. These cuts clearly reflect the President's policies,[1] and had Congress not opposed even deeper cuts, the damages would have been worse still. Nuclear energy is the Administration's choice energy source. The President would have the nation grow more and more dependent on fission-based nuclear power, a very troubled energy source indeed.

The vision that emerges from these budgets and the policies they reflect is not one most Americans share. A recent NBC poll, for example, shows that the American public overwhelmingly believes that "the future energy needs of the United States would be better served...by more conservation and expansion of other energy sources," with greatest popular support for solar energy development.[2] The poll also found that a majority (56 percent) of Americans believe that no new nuclear plants should be built in this country. A second, exhaustive study by researchers at the Washington State University found that "the public does not show the same enthusiasm for nuclear energy as the Reagan Administration or the nuclear industry, and simultaneously appears most

TRENDS IN FEDERAL ENERGY FUNDING

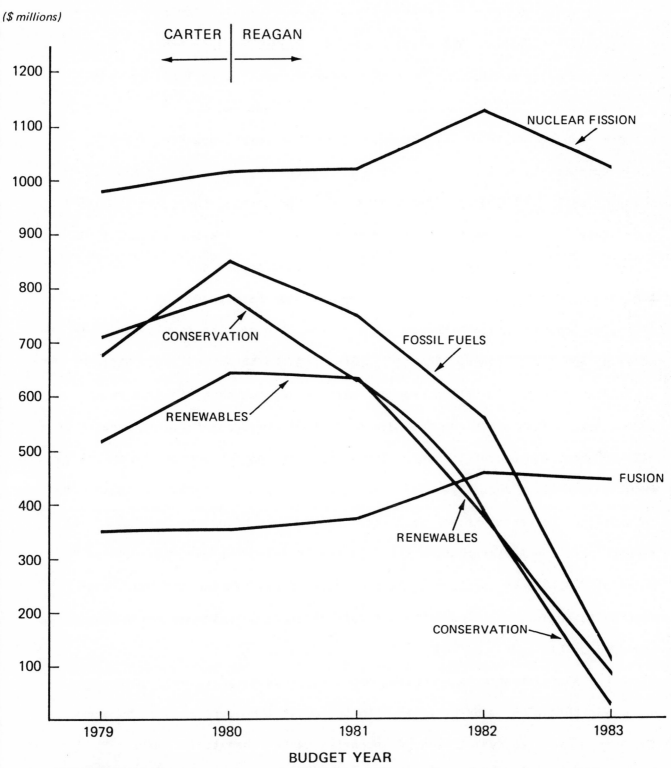

($ millions)

CARTER | REAGAN

1200

1100 — NUCLEAR FISSION

1000

900

800

CONSERVATION

700 — FOSSIL FUELS

600

RENEWABLES

500

FUSION

400

RENEWABLES

300

200

CONSERVATION

100

1979   1980   1981   1982   1983

BUDGET YEAR

SOURCE: Subcommittee on Energy Conservation and Power, Committee on Energy and Commerce, U.S. House of Representatives

43

receptive to the very energy sources--especially solar and conservation--which the administration is deemphasizing."[3]

The Administration's energy policies clash even with its own avowed free-market principles. The White House is pushing for expanded reliance on nuclear energy, even though a host of unresolved safety, reliability, and waste-disposal problems make nuclear energy ever less economic.[4] Rather than allowing the market to decide the case of nuclear power, however, the Administration is seeking to subsidize it directly by allocating public funds and indirectly by relaxing safeguards aimed at protecting the public health and safety. At the same time, President Reagan is withdrawing virtually all federal support for market-improving programs that supply consumers and American business with investment information and assistance.

The Administration's energy policies are at odds with Americans' concerns about the economy, the environment and the threat of war. White House energy proposals will worsen our already serious economic problems. U.S. energy bills have risen from 8.5 percent of the Gross National Product in 1973 to about 15 percent in 1980. Total expenditures for energy now amount to about $400 billion annually--nearly $2000 for every man, woman, and child. By subsidizing nuclear power and synthetic fuels and ignoring the message of the marketplace, the Administration will greatly increase the economic burden borne by U.S. energy consumers. If they have to pay needlessly high prices to meet basic needs, consumers will have less discretionary income and a lower standard of living.

The Administration's "produce, produce, produce" philosophy only compounds this problem by directing limited capital resources into the search for ever more expensive oil and gas supplies rather than to far more cost-effective investments in energy efficiency. As billions of dollars are channeled into uneconomic and unproductive technologies, less capital will be available for stimulating economic growth, spurring technological innovation, and increasing industrial productivity. Like the enormous budget deficits that the Administration is proposing, these demands for capital will generate upward pressures on interest rates, exacerbating inflation and thwarting economic recovery.

The Administration's energy policies threaten the environment, an issue that continues to rank high in importance with the American public. By continuing support and subsidies for synthetic fuels, the Administration is jeopardizing the environmental health of states that produce coal and oil shale. Synthetic fuel plants pose many poorly understood environmental and occupational hazards ranging from air- and water pollutants to toxic wastes.[5] Common sense dictates a go-slow approach. Yet, the Aministration has approved the subsidized construction of synfuel plants and has severely cut the Environmental Protection Agency just when its regulatory oversight is most needed.[6]

Serious socioeconomic impacts from synfuels development can also be expected in the western states, which contain most of our coal and oil shale. Without careful planning, the heritage and character of the West will be irretrievably lost to boom towns and industrial development.[7] Implementation of the Administration's proposed programs would undo a decade's progress toward improving the quality of America's air, water, and soil, and toward maintaining the productivity of its other natural resources.

Finally, the Administration's energy program increases the risks to national and global security, thereby ignoring the growing concern among Americans over the threat of nuclear war. Its commitments to plutonium reprocesssing and the Clinch River Breeder Reactor increase the likelihood of international nuclear weapons proliferation. And its retreat from energy conservation and solar energy development increases the likelihood we will go to war to maintain access to foreign oil supplies, most notably in the Middle East.

The following pages set out in more detail the elements of the Administration's solar, conservation and nuclear energy proposals and the reasons why they are largely counterproductive in dealing with our underlying energy problems. (The Reagan Administration's reckless leasing of public lands, as well as other actions related to developing and using fossil fuels, will be covered in the forthcoming report, "Indictment: The Case Against the Reagan Environmental Record.") Section III sketches an alternative energy program--one that would help the United States meet its energy needs in the most cost-effective way possible and support such other important national goals as economic growth, national security, full employment, environmental protection and social justice.

II. PORTRAIT OF A FACT-BLIND ENERGY POLICY

Over the past fourteen months the Administration has rewritten U.S. energy policy. Radical changes--from drastic budget cutbacks at the Department of Energy to the wholesale revision of environmental regulations--have touched every major energy-related federal program.

At What Price Nuclear Power?

In October of 1981, President Reagan called for a major federal effort to revive the nearly moribund U.S. nuclear power industry. According to the policy statement, "One of the best potential sources of new electrical energy supplies in the coming decades is nuclear power," though "the Federal Government has created a regulatory environment that is forcing many utilities to rule out nuclear power as a source of new generating capacity,..." "Nuclear power," the statement reads, "has become entangled in a morass of regulations that do not enhance safety but that do cause extensive licensing delays and economic uncertainty." The Administration concludes that we "must move rapidly to eliminate unnecessary government barriers to efficient utilization of our abundant, economical resources of coal and uranium."[8]

The Administration obviously believes that Federal regulations--not substantive technical, safety, and economic problems--have caused the demise of the nuclear industry. Its proposals for dealing with this perceived problem include reducing federal safety regulation over nuclear power, constructing the Clinch River plutonium breeder reactor, encouraging private firms to reprocess spent fuel (possibly for sale to the government, which could use the the recovered plutonium for nuclear weapons production), "swiftly" deploying the means of storing radioactive wastes, and launching a multi-million dollar propaganda campaign aimed at improving nuclear power's public image.

The Administration's zeal for nuclear power emerges clearly from its budget proposals. Nuclear energy constitutes the only important energy program spared deep cuts from the Reagan budget axe. In the President's 1983 budget proposal, nuclear energy—fission and fusion—would receive a total of $1.4 billion, and nuclear research and commercialization programs would account for 87 percent of the Department of Energy's research funds for energy technology.[9]

The irony is that the Reagan Administration's commitment to "reviving the nuclear industry" comes at a time when energy economists have all but declared the industry dead because of the bleak outlook for new orders. A decline in the growth rate of electricity demand, increases in interest rates, cost overruns, construction delays, heavy competition in capital markets, and a growing realization among utilities of the economic and safety risks posed by reactors have resulted in a five-year de facto moratorium on reactor orders and the cancellations of plans for more than 81 reactors, more than now operate in the United States.[10] In fact, the nuclear industry's only current U.S. business consists of a backlog of orders from the early 1970s, when plants could still be built for less than $1 billion apiece and nuclear electricity could still compete economically with coal-generated electricity—as it never will again.

Utilities with heavy investments in nuclear power are faring worse than other electric utilities, few of which still enjoy Wall Street's blessing since their return on investment dropped to an uninviting 11 percent. Investors are increasingly wary of what has been called a "business that can lose $2 billion in half an hour." In the last six months, utilities have scrapped investments in 13 large reactors to keep their losses in the hundreds of millions instead of billions, and thus restore their financial credibility.[11]

Regulatory Reform--A Solution In Search of a Problem

In October of 1981, the Administration called for measures to streamline nuclear plant licensing, citing a need to cut costs associated with construction and licensing delays. Following the Administration's lead, the nuclear industry placed full-page newspaper ads claiming that 33 nuclear plants could be licensed over the next two years if only the federal bureaucracy could be prodded into action. Supposedly, such administrative bungling costs consumers billions of dollars per year. The facts say otherwise, however. Nuclear Regulatory Commissioner Victor Gilinsky contends that no more than 20 of the 33 plants are likely even to be completed within this period.[12] And the most recent NRC report to the House Appropriations Subcommittee (the so-called Bevill report) lists only one plant as likely to be finished before its license is approved, and even then for only two months.[13]

What the Administration fails to acknowledge is that the construction of many nuclear plants is being delayed or deferred for reasons other than regulatory requirements. The real reasons include reduced growth rates for power, difficulties in financing, construction mistakes, late parts delivery, and labor problems.[14] To misconstrue these cancellations, delays, and deferrals as products of a "morass of regulations" is to mislead the public.

If the Reagan proposals are adopted, the real problems that plague the industry--poor management and lack of quality control--may well go untreated. As Nunzio J. Palladino, the new chairman of the NRC said in a December 1981 speech to the Atomic Industrial Forum:[15]

> If the nuclear industry does not do its part, no amount of
> regulatory reform will save it from the consequences of its own
> failures to achieve the quality of construction and plant operations
> it must have for its own well-being and for the safety of the
> public it serves. Based on quality assurance failures that have

recently come to light, I am not convinced that all of the industry has been doing its part...Their deficiencies in quality assurance are inexcusable...There have been lapses of many kinds--in design analyses resulting in built-in design errors; in poor construction practices; in falsified documents; in harassment of quality control personnel; and in inadequate training of reactor operators.

Nuclear Bombs From Nuclear Power

In his October statement on nuclear power, President Reagan also lifted the ban on commercial reprocessing of spent nuclear fuel. In so doing, he ignored important lessons from the history of the reprocessing issue. In October of 1976, President Ford determined that commercial reprocessing of spent nuclear fuel, and the subsequent use of the recovered plutonium in existing nuclear power plants, should be held in abeyance until the adequacy of non-proliferation safeguards could be demonstrated. In April of 1977, President Carter went one step farther and deferred indefinitely the commercial reprocessing of spent fuel and the introduction of the plutonium breeder reactor. Both Presidents recognized that worldwide reprocessing could accelerate the spread of nuclear weapons by opening up trade in plutonium, the explosive material from which nuclear bombs can be made. Apparently, President Reagan does not share the same concern.

Commercial reprocessing is widely recognized by the nuclear industry as an uneconomic enterprise. With uranium prices falling, there is little or no economic advantage to using the recovered plutonium as fuel for light-water reactors.[16] Nor can reprocessing be justified for use in plutonium breeder reactors, whose commercial prospects are remote indeed. In fact, within days of the Administration's announcement of its support for reprocessing, Allied Corporation--part owner with the General Atomic Company of the partially completed reprocessing facility in Barnwell, South Carolina--announced that it

was writing the facility off its books.[17] Clearly, the Administration's
position cannot be justified on economic grounds: left to itself, reprocessing
would simply not survive in a free market.

Motives other than energy production have been suggested as
justification for the Administration's policy. One is using the plutonium
recovered during reprocessing to support the greatly stepped up production of
nuclear weapons initiated by the Administration.[18]

Using the plutonium from commercial spent fuel to build nuclear weapons
would break down the strategically and diplomatically critical distinction
between the civilian and military uses of nuclear materials. It would also
pose the risk that radioactive waste management and disposal would be removed
completely from civilian oversight, with the subsequent loss of NRC licensing,
public comment and review.

The gravity of this radical change in policy is widely recognized. In
July of 1981, the Natural Resources Defense Council charged that "the
Administration is embarking upon a perilous program to turn commercial nuclear
power plants around this country into bomb making factories...which is totally
inconsistent with 30 years of American efforts to assure that 'peaceful'
nuclear materials and technology are not directed to the manufacture of atomic
bombs."[19] Paul Leventhal, President of "The Nuclear Club, Inc.," an
organization opposing the spread of nuclear weapons, told the New York Times
that this breech would "render meaningless [those] efforts by the United
States to dissuade foreign governments from using their commercial nuclear
facilities to provide a weapons option."[20] Even a member of the American
Nuclear Energy Council objected to what he saw as a "public relations
disaster." "We've spent years," the Council official said, "reassuring the
public that nuclear power is separate from nuclear weapons."[21]

The importance of preventing the spread of nuclear weapons seems to elude the Reagan Administration, which is abandoning policies that recent administrations regarded as essentials to a sound nuclear policy. In place of the example the United States set by enforcing the reprocessing ban, President Reagan intends to rely upon handshake diplomacy bolstered by International Atomic Energy Agency monitoring, widely recognized as inadequate to the task.[22] Nothing keeps this approach from disintegrating into mere international business deals, with government going to bat for U.S. nuclear firms rather than serving the broader interests of the American people or world peace.

If the United States turns its commercial power plants into production facilities for nuclear weapons materials, what is to keep other nations from following suit? An enhanced weapons build-up would inevitably follow, as would a greatly increased risk of their use.

The Breeder Reactor--Unnecessary and Uneconomic

Perhaps the most extreme waste of federal energy dollars that the Administration has proposed is funding for the Clinch River Breeder Reactor. This highly controversial project, first proposed in 1970 with a price tag of $500 million, to date represents a billion-dollar investment, and the pre-construction estimate of its cost now stands at $3.5 billion.[23] The Reagan Administration has called for $194 million for the Clinch River Breeder in 1982 and $252 million in 1983.[24] Though apparently now favoring construction of the plant, in 1981 the prominent nuclear advocate Edward Teller described the Clinch River reactor as already "technically obsolescent" and "thoroughly inconsistent with badly needed economy in government."[25]

The Administration's rationale for funding the Clinch River Breeder Reactor sounds simple: the nuclear economy would become self-perpetuating if it shifted its base from reliance upon existing light-water reactors to reliance on breeder reactors, which are more efficient users of fuel. But self-perpetuating at what cost? According to a recent study by the Department of Energy's Los Alamos Scientific Laboratory, uranium prices--currently around $25 per pound--would have to reach about $165 per pound for the breeder to compete with light-water reactors.[26] Nor is Los Alamos a lone voice in the debate over the breeder's economic future. Recent House hearings indicate that with the use of more uranium-efficient light-water reactors the break-even price would have to rise to at least $200 per pound.[27] The Wall Street Journal predicts that breeder reactors will not compete economically until "2030 or beyond."[28] Even David Stockman (as a Congressman) called the Clinch River Breeder Reactor "totally incompatible with our free market approach to energy policy," and so it remains.[29] And in late 1981, DOE's own Energy Research Advisory Board advised Energy Secretary James Edwards to cut off funding for Clinch River on grounds that the project is "not an urgent priority" and that the United States has enough coal and uranium to satisfy electrical demand until at least 2020.[30]

The poor economic outlook for the breeder is vividly confirmed by the European experience with advanced breeders. Five years ago, France was committed to building six 1200-megawatt "Superphenix" breeder reactors. As the first of these power plants nears completion, however, it has become clear that high construction costs make the breeder far too costly, about twice as expensive as French light-water reactors.[31] As a consequence, the French have made no further commitment to constructing the five remaining breeders. In West Germany, the Parliament will decide this year whether the 300-megawatt demonstration breeder, which has been under construction for 8 years, will be completed. And the United Kingdom has no present plans to build a commerical-scale breeder reactor.

Even the U.S. nuclear industry is unwilling to risk its capital on breeders. Its commitment to the Clinch River Breeder still stands at the original $257 million that it agreed to contribute in 1970, when the nuclear venture was being cost-shared on a 50-50 basis.[32] Only if taxpayers end up covering more than 90 percent of the project and bear the burden of a 13.5 percent "real" annual rate of cost increase in building nuclear reactors will the industry buy into breeders.[33]

In encouraging the deployment of breeder reactors, the Administration also ignores the threat they pose to world peace. Consider that each year a single breeder reactor reprocessing plant would discharge enough plutonium to make 10,000 nuclear weapons—about equal to the total U.S. arsenal of strategic nuclear weapons.[34] A global economy utilizing several thousand breeder and light-water nuclear power plants would need perhaps sixty fuel-reprocessing plants, each year reprocessing enough plutonium to make 200,000 nuclear weapons.[35] Can there be any doubt that the circulation of this much plutonium will hasten the spread of nuclear weapons? And that with their spread their use will become more likely?

Aiding the Spread of Nuclear Weapons

The Administration's insensitivity to the link between nuclear power and nuclear weapons also reveals itself in a number of its other nuclear power related policies. During the past year, the United States has virtually abandoned its tough stance on slowing the spread of "sensitive" nuclear technologies—those that could be used to help make nuclear weapons. Instead, it has taken a weak position based on its leverage as a "reliable nuclear supplier." During the past year it has lifted the ban on supplying military and economic aid to Pakistan, a country known to be developing nuclear weapons. Having softened its stance, the United States also has under review policies to[36]

—Export classified technology for enriching uranium, technology that would directly allow the acquisition of weapons-grade nuclear materials, and

—Allow India to reprocess U.S.-supplied nuclear power plant fuel, even though that nation refuses to subject its entire fuel cycle to international safeguards.

The Administration expresses legitimate concern about the strategic arms race and the growing threat of nuclear war between the superpowers. Yet, its various nuclear policies could enable many non-nuclear nations--including some that are politically unstable and reckless--to become major nuclear powers.

Radioactive Wastes--Rushing to Failure

The Administration's position on radioactive wastes is that "...there is no question that technically acceptable means of disposal exist..."[37] In fact, in October of 1981, President Reagan directed DOE Secretary Edwards to work "...closely with industry and state governments, to proceed swiftly toward deployment of means of storing and disposing of commercial high-level radioactive waste."[38] The stark facts, however, are that no proven means of safe disposal exist and that many of the technical and scientific problems of waste disposal are just beginning to be addressed. These problems have been outlined in several recent reports. The U.S. Geological Survey concluded that "the difficulties and uncertainties connected with the geologic disposal of high-level waste" represent "significant potential stumbling blocks that need critical attention."[39] The Survey's report describes in detail the areas of needed research, which has only recently begun to be undertaken. Similarly, a year-long government-wide study undertaken during the Carter Administration concluded that the waste problem is one "whose resolution will clearly require an unprecedented extension of capabilities in rock mechanics, geochemistry, hydrogeology, and long-term predictions of seismicity, volcanism, and climate."[40]

Gradually, progress is being made, but important technical problems still await resolution. Questions remain about the reliability of long-term geological predictions, the consequences of interaction between water and the host rock in a repository, the relative value of different waste forms, and the potential for identifying acceptable geological sites.

The Administration proposes pushing ahead with the burial of radioactive wastes before an adequate scientific basis for doing so has been established. But without a credible scientific foundation and without public support, it should be prepared for another technological fiasco like the Lyons, Kansas, project--the original "demonstration" of nuclear waste disposal technology, which had to be abandoned in 1972 because of poor planning and technical incompetence.[41] Developing safe disposal technology will take time, and burying wastes prematurely could prove to be dangerous and costly. It is a job better done well than fast, whatever the industry may believe about "out of sight, out of mind."

The Federal Hard-Sell of Nuclear Power

Rather than dealing directly with the substantive safety and reliability problems plaguing the nuclear industry, the Reagan Administration has proposed costly and largely irrelevant programs, buttressed by a multi-million dollar federally funded public relations campaign.[42]

In late 1981, a lengthy and startling DOE memo was leaked to the press. In it were proposals to promote nuclear power through a series of "public information" activities. Op-ed articles, interviews, media appearances by DOE spokesmen, ghost-written articles for periodicals, briefings for the financial community, joint PR efforts with nuclear trade organizations, support for preparing pro-nuclear materials for use in community and campus forums--these and many other activities paid for with public funds were proposed to help change public opinion on the nuclear power issue. Indeed, DOE even proposed enlisting the National Academy of Sciences to "play a role in nuclear energy public information."

The Administration's proposed pro-nuclear PR campaign is aimed at a public growing increasingly skeptical of nuclear power. According to a poll taken last November by NBC and the Associated Press, when asked to choose between conservation and other energy sources, and nuclear power, 63 percent of Americans polled picked the former, and only 18 percent picked nuclear.[43] Other polls show that between 90 and 95 percent vigorously support solar energy, regardless of their position in the conservation versus nuclear debate.[44] Ranking their preferences, Americans placed nuclear power last.[45]

*   *   *

The Last Word on Nuclear Power

Nuclear power's demise in the marketplace reflects reduced electric growth rates, rapidly escalating capital costs, and unsolved problems related to plant safety and radioactive waste management. The technology was rushed into being by federal subsidies--chief among them, the Price Anderson Act, which essentially absolved the nuclear industry of liability for major accidents.[46] Without this subsidy the debate over the dangers inherent in nuclear power would not have persisted even this long because, quite simply, the nuclear era would never have begun.

Nothing that the Administration has proposed will deal constructively with these underlying problems. Indeed, the problems plaguing the industry

57

could be made worse by ignoring them, or "demonstrating" solutions when none exist. "Streamlining the licensing process" when there are essentially no plants being delayed by the regulatory process, encouraging fuel reprocessing when it is patently uneconomical and poses a major proliferation threat, building the Clinch River Breeder Reactor when breeders are many decades from being economically viable, proposing deployment of partially developed waste disposal technology, and attempting to whitewash nuclear problems through a federal PR program--these actions serve neither the long-term national interest nor the interest of the nuclear industry. The nation would do far better to pursue energy efficiency, solar energy, and other economically and environmentally attractive energy options that the Administration has so far neglected.

The Reagan Conservation Initiative: Dismantling the Federal Program

When the President stated shortly after his election that conservation meant being too hot in summer and too cold in winter, many dismissed the remark as mere rhetoric. Now, we know it was not. The budget for energy conservation has been reduced 97 percent since the President took office, from $925 million to a proposed $22 million for fiscal year 1983.[47] In the Administration's listing of the worst 20 federal regulations, two conservation regulations--the Building Energy Performance Standards and the Residential Conservation Service--were included.[48] And two other congressionally mandated regulations, appliance efficiency standards and new automobile efficiency standards, are likely to be weakened. Finally, the Administration slated for elimination the existing 15 percent residential energy-conservation tax credit, a proposal that was withdrawn only after 266 members of the House and 62 members of the Senate signed a resolution opposing such a move.[49]

Regrettably, the President's view that efficiency means deprivation and "doing without" demonstrates a fundamental misunderstanding of the term. Efficiency means doing more with less, and not simply doing with less. It means meeting our needs for lighting, warmth, mobility and industrial process energy in the most economic and efficient manner possible. Conservation involves technology just as much as supply alternatives, and requires research, investment, marketing, and consumer acceptance. And like supply technologies, conservation technologies are also evolving. In the future, homes will require less energy for heating and cooling, automobiles will use much less fuel, and factories will produce the same quantity of goods with much less energy. In short, conservation means increasing energy productivity, and therefore national productivity--a goal that the Administration has every reason to embrace.

The Administration's disdain for increasing energy efficiency flies in the face of indisputable evidence that efficiency represents the cheapest, safest, and quickest way to meet U.S. energy needs. Reports issued by such diverse groups as the Solar Energy Research Institute, the National Academy of Sciences, the Mellon Institute's Energy Productivity Center, the Harvard Business School, and others all endorse conservation as a necessary element of a sound energy future.[50] Indeed, these studies establish that "efficiency supplies" are currently available at prices equivalent to yesteryear's oil prices--$1 to $25 per barrel.[51] They also demonstrate that with an aggressive program to improve energy efficiency, U.S. energy consumption in the year 2000 could actually be reduced below what it is today.[52]

Energy conservation has become critical to the health of our economy, as well as our national security. Between 1973 and 1980, U.S. energy consumption rose by a total of only 2 percent.[53] Over this same period, real Gross National Product--corrected for inflation--rose by 18 percent.[54] Thus, almost

90 percent of the economic growth during these eight years was supported through increases in national energy productivity and only 10 percent through the introduction of additional energy sources.[55] The temporary world oil glut we are now enjoying, along with the price stability it has brought, is due largely to conservation efforts.

Its conservation policy shows that the Administration misunderstands the existing energy market in two fundamental ways. First, the free market is not perfect, and as a result billions of dollars of cost-effective efficiency investments are not being made.[56] And, second, the U.S. energy market has been substantially distorted over the decades to favor conventional energy production over conservation. Tax incentives for energy production, for example, outweigh those for conservation by eight to one.[57]

Market Imperfections

High energy prices can induce energy consumers to conserve, but only if they have access to information on how to do so. Right after the Arab Oil Embargo, energy consumers began to implement the "easy" conservation--they turned off unneeded lights and insulated their hot water heaters. But, in the years since, they have had to turn to more substantial conservation measures, and here they have encountered problems. Much of the information on conservation is conflicting and consumers get little help deciding what to believe and what to do. Naturally, many choose to do nothing rather than risk making a mistake.

Congress has attempted in the last few years to meet this need for consumer information. The Residential Conservation Service (RCS) was created to compel utilities to provide energy audits of the homes of interested customers.[58] Appliance labeling for energy efficiency was mandated, as has been done for automobiles.[59] Seminars and brochures were prepared by the

Department of Energy on how to improve energy efficiency in industrial and transportation systems. While it is difficult to gauge the overall effect of these programs on energy consumption, consumer response has been quite favorable. Yet, all of these programs are slated for extinction by the Reagan Administration.

Apart from the question of information, energy consumers can reduce their demands for energy only if conservation technologies are available. Yet, unless adequate resources are devoted to their research and development, such technologies will never become available.

In a number of areas, the resources devoted to conservation research and development are woefully inadequate. The reasons are severalfold. Some industries, such as as the building industry, are diffuse and have no centralized organization to support research. Others are in such poor financial health that they have no capital to devote to conservation. Still other industries will not invest in research because the payoffs are too far in the future. Under such circumstances, many opportunities to improve national energy efficiency will be lost unless the government provides the needed support for research on new conservation technologies. Such energy efficient products as heat-pump water heaters and solid-state ballasts that improve the efficiency of fluorescent lights would not have appeared on the market nearly as soon as they did without federally supported research.[60] Congress has appropriated funds for such research, but the Reagan Administration plans to eliminate these important programs.[61]

In addition to a lack of adequate information and research, there are other factors inhibiting efficient operation of the marketplace. Chief among these is the failure of many institutions to accept energy conservation. For example, while about one third of all Americans live in rental housing, a lack of incentives keeps both tenants and landlords from making conservation improvements. Tenants are reluctant to pay for improvements in the landlord's building, while landlords can simply pass through fuel costs in the rent and so have little incentive to make efficiency improvements. This is a serious problem, and one that the government could help solve. Unfortunately, the Administration has made no move to do so.

Nor is the building sector alone in facing institutional barriers. While industry has made impressive progress over the past few years, it has by no means made all the improvements that are cost effective. A study carried out by the Department of Energy last year estimated that less than one fifth of the reduction in industrial energy consumption (measured per unit of industrial output) has been due to investments in energy efficiency. Most industrial conservation efforts have been limited to "housekeeping improvements" or to shifts away from products that require a great deal of energy to manufacture. The reasons for this are simple. Corporations face many of the same problems that homeowners experience--high interest rates, lack of credible sources of information, and other competing priorities, such as attempting to maintain market share with new products. Accordingly, industrial decision-makers have tended to apply more stringent investment criteria to conservation improvements than they do to other investment opportunities. As a result, many otherwise attractive investments in energy efficiency have not been made. The federal government could--through information dissemination, for example--begin to deal with these problems but` under the Administration it isn't.

Present electric rate structures in many states also pose a barrier to efficient market operation. New power plants are very costly to build and the power from them will be more expensive than power from existing plants. If electric rate structures fail to reflect the higher costs of meeting new growth in demand, consumers--particularly those with large and growing demands--will receive price signals that encourage them to use more electricity than is economically efficient. The epitome of this problem is the outmoded "declining block" rate structure, whereby price per unit of power declines with increasing use. New rate structures that encourage the efficient use of electricity are being considered in many states and have been adopted in some. Such rate structure reform should be accelerated so that unnecessary powerplant construction and the resulting misallocation of scarce capital can be minimized.

The market has still other imperfections. It does not adequately address the "non-economic" needs of our country. For example, the market does not take into account our national security needs. Fifteen percent of our oil today is imported from the unstable Middle East, more than was imported during the Arab Oil Embargo.[62] Relying solely on the market will not reduce our dependence on that region quickly enough. Nor does the marketplace presently provide for environmental quality or public safety. It does not take into account the risks of altering the climate from burning fossil fuels or the threat of weapons proliferation from nuclear power.

Finally, the Administration's laissez-faire attitude toward conservation simply ignores the plight of low-income families that lack credit or capital. These Americans are falling farther and farther behind despite heroic, and sometimes dangerous, attempts to use less energy.[63] Energy expenditures in the United States have topped $400 billion a year. Millions of households now find that they must set aside 20 to 30 percent of their monthly income to pay for energy. And in some months that percentage approaches 100 percent for households on fixed or declining incomes. Yet, the Administration has proposed ending all funding for the Low-Income Weatherization Program, a program designed to provide permanent relief to 12 million low-income families by weatherizing their homes. The market will not provide for these families.

Energy Subsidies

The ultimate hypocrisy of the Reagan Administration's free market rhetoric is that this Administration is as guilty as its predecessors of distorting the market through government subsidies. These subsidies flow to the production of conventional sources of energy, artificially lowering costs and encouraging the use of fuels rather than investments in efficiency improvements or in renewable energy. Estimates of these government subsidies range from $10 billion to $16 billion annually.[64] In contrast, federal conservation subsidies--most of which the Reagan Administration would like to eliminate--amount to only $1 billion to $2 billion annually.[65]

Production subsidies take many forms. The nuclear industry receives subsidies for research and development, foreign reactor sales, the exploration, production, and enrichment of uranium, radioactive waste management, the development of the breeder reactor and commercial reprocessing, and insurance against nuclear accidents. And the fossil fuels industry receives subsidies for synthetic fuels development, oil and gas exploration and drilling, foreign oil production, and oil depletion.[66] Were these subsidies eliminated, conservation would be better able to compete in the marketplace with energy production.

The Reagan Administration has made no attempt to eliminate these subsidies, moving instead to further distort the market.[67] For example, the electric utility industry has come in for special help from the Administration. The 1981 tax cuts included an incentive to induce investment in the stocks of certain utilities. Investors in these companies will be able to receive up to $750 in tax-free dividends. Ironically, some utilities have indicated that the new law will not help them much because these utilities pay almost no federal taxes. (This problem, however, is also addressed in the tax bill, which allows the sale of unusable tax credits.)

Another tax concession, this one initiated by the Federal Energy Regulatory Commission (FERC), assures that utilities can keep those tax breaks associated with the sale of wholesale power, rather than sharing them with customers. Still another pending proposal, strongly endorsed by the Reagan-appointed FERC Chairman, would allow utilities much greater latitude in obtaining a return on investments in power plants that are still under construction. FERC has also proposed substantially reducing reporting requirements so that utilities will have to supply less of the cost information that is crucial in the scrutiny of rate requests. The Department of Energy's national electricity policy project is expected to develop still other special privileges for the utility industry.

One of the few energy tax subsidies the Administration has proposed eliminating is—true to form—for conservation, the business energy credit.

Solar Eclipse

Two nation-wide polls conducted during the Presidential campaign—one by Gallup, the other by Roper and Cantril—revealed that more Americans want to see renewable energy used to meet U.S. energy demand than any other option.[68] This popular support should come as no surprise. Used wisely, power from the sun, wind, falling water and plants is gentle to the environment. Its use presents few of the economic and safety risks posed by the fossil and nuclear alternatives.

The Rawest Deal

Although President Reagan has claimed that solar energy is "exotic" and that solar technologies are "not viable alternatives to oil, coal, and nuclear power," the evidence to the contrary is overwhelming. According to A New Prosperity (a Solar Energy Research Institute report that the Administration tried to suppress), 20 to 30 percent of U.S. energy demand in the year 2000 could be met by renewable resources, assuming the country follows an energy-efficient path.[69] (Renewable resources, mostly wood and hydropower, now meet about 6 percent of U.S. energy needs.) Such a future would not be one of deprivation. Indeed, the SERI analysts assumed an increase of 45 percent in per capita income and a real 80 percent increase in GNP over the remainder of the century.[70] Similar conclusions were reached by the Harvard Business School's Energy Project.

The facts the Reagan Administration denies add up to a strong case for increased support for solar energy technology development. Yet, three months after he was elected, President Reagan called for a 69 percent reduction, from $576 million to $193 million, in the solar budget.[71] Six months later, he proposed a solar budget of $73 million for 1983—about 92 cents per American home, each of which spends an average of about $750 on household energy purchases each year.[72] (As part of these cuts the Administration has fired 300 of the 800 employees of the Solar Energy Research Institute, the nation's only national laboratory focused on conservation and renewable energy resources.)

The Administration justified the solar budget cuts on grounds that government energy subsidies should be eliminated and that the solar tax credits now in effect provide sufficient incentives. But the White House's subsequent actions proved the hypocrisy of the energy plan. For while the Administration wants to slash solar energy funding, it proposed a 36 percent increase in the fiscal 1982 nuclear budget, and accepted $12 billion of additional tax benefits for oil companies. Moreover, after the energy budget was approved by Congress (which added over $100 million to the President's solar request), the Administration then targeted the solar tax credits for repeal. The attempt was stymied by a joint resolution of the House and Senate. But the latest Reagan budget again targets the solar business energy credits for repeal, while maintaining such incentives for the oil industry as the special depletion allowance and deductions for "intangible" drilling expenses, incentives that are projected to cost the U.S. Treasury $6.4 billion in fiscal year 1983.[73]

Besides attacking solar programs and tax credits, the Administration has sought to undermine some of the federal laws and regulations that currently affect solar technologies. As mentioned, Congress rejected the Administration's effort to destroy the Residential Conservation Service Program, which requires utilities to provide energy audits for customers. But despite support for RCS in Congress, the Administration has proposed radically changing the RCS regulations so that in virtually no instances will auditors be able to suggest solar applications.[74] The White House has also supported legislation to "deregulate" small hydropower projects at most potential sites, creating environmental, water, and land management problems even as FERC is being deluged with applications for project permits. Although the prospects for this legislation are not bright, the Administration has already weakened FERC environmental safeguards by drastically reducing the staff that does the basic river basin planning needed in hydropower licensing.

The White House has also supported legislation to weaken the Public Utility Regulatory Policies Act, part of which requires utilities to purchase excess electricity from small power producers and cogenerators.[75] The law addresses the major problem that private entrepreneurs of small-scale hydroelectric dams, wind energy systems, and cogenerators face--integrating with utility grids. Weakening the law could allow the utilities to maintain a monopoly on power production and discourage the development of decentralized energy sources. The Congress has so far rejected the Administration's efforts.

Besides enhancing national security by reducing oil imports, a broad-based program of federal support for renewable resources provides a firm hedge against inflation. Once installed, solar systems require no fuels, the rising costs of which today contribute heavily to inflation. Renewable resources also pose far fewer environmental hazards than coal and nuclear power (particularly climate changes induced by the atmospheric buildup of carbon dioxide resulting from the burning of fossil fuels)[76] and threats to world peace from international commerce in plutonium. Difficult to quantify, these benefits--like those of conservation--are assigned no value in the present market structure despite their obvious importance.

What's Needed

The type of federal assistance needed by renewable resources varies from technology to technology. In most cases, federal tax credits are needed to compensate for the subsidies to conventional fuels and to stimulate production and sales that will help drive down costs. These credits, which the Reagan Administration has threatened to abolish, also help compensate for the relatively high up-front costs of purchasing solar equipment. For consumers unable to purchase renewable energy systems for their homes (solar collectors, wind turbines, photovoltaic cells, and the like) or unable to use tax credits, Congress established the Energy Conservation and Solar Energy Bank in 1980 to provide low-interest loans to low- and moderate-income people. This institution has also come under attack from the Administration, which has fired the Bank's staff, withheld implementing regulations, proposed rescinding funds, and refused to start up the Bank despite clear direction from Congress to proceed.

Besides financing assistance, solar information for energy users is needed. Especially hard-pressed for information is the building sector, which tends to be fragmented and slow to innovate. Programs to accelerate the flow of accurate solar information to homeowners, developers, and the owners of commercial buildings can remove one of the major barriers to effective consumer action--the lack of credible information on what works and what doesn't. Providing such information costs relatively little and can measurably improve the operation of market forces. Yet, the Administration is reducing the distribution of such materials.

Finally, for some solar technologies, other types of support may be warranted. In the case of photovoltaics, a rapidly developing technology that converts sunlight directly into electricity, the compelling need is to bring down system costs. If, according to a joint report by the Solar Lobby and the Solar Energy Industries Association, the U.S. photovoltaics program's momentum can be sustained, the equivalent of 330,000 barrels of oil a day can be displaced within two decades by using photovoltaic devices.[77] One effective way to bring down costs is through a federal purchasing program, which can provide the volume demand needed to justify mass production. Unfortunately, the Reagan Administration shows no interest such a program.

Supporters of renewable energy simply want the federal government to give emerging renewable technologies a fair shake, either by eliminating all subsidies to all energy sources or by providing a balanced energy program to all energy sources. Offering little more than free-enterprise rhetoric, the Administration is instead perpetuating lopsided and counterproductive subsidies to conventional fuel producers and passing over our best hope for new supplies of clean, safe, and reliable energy.

III. TOWARD A RATIONAL ENERGY POLICY

A rational U.S. energy policy requires realistic assessments of both our future energy needs and the energy sources available to meet them. A policy should strive for economic efficiency, meeting the nation's requirements for energy services--lighting, warmth, mobility, and so forth--as cost-effectively as possible, while taking into account the economic and other risks and advantages posed by alternative energy technologies.

A national energy policy should also complement the achievement of such national goals as enhancing national security, sustaining economic growth, safeguarding environmental quality, and increasing employment. And it should ensure that low-income Americans can meet their basic energy needs.

Such a policy can be designed. Indeed, its essential elements have been described in numerous studies since the word "energy" became linked with "crisis." Summarized here, they stand as an alternative to the piecemeal and counterproductive proposals that the Reagan Administration has advanced during the past 14 months.

Increasing National Energy Efficiency

Increasing national energy efficiency should be the highest immediate priority, rather than the lowest. As published studies document, cost-effective conservation technology now available can continue to substantially reduce our needs for oil, gas, and electricity for many years at "effective fuel costs" far below those of new and existing energy sources.

In addition to being cost-effective, conservation improvements enhance national security enormously. Indeed, between 1977 and 1981, conservation improvements led to a 33 percent reduction in oil imports.[78] What's more, these improvements have come about far more quickly and inexpensively and with far fewer environmental impacts than would be possible with any program based on synthetic fuels or nuclear energy.

Focusing our national investment policy on making our industrial processes and consumer products more energy efficient will keep U.S. businesses more competitive with foreign producers and increase domestic employment. Fewer jobs will be lost to foreign competition if American producers develop more energy-efficient cars, refrigerators, and other consumer goods. As it is, many traditionally strong American industries can no longer endure the flood of more energy-efficient products manufactured abroad. As a result, more and more American workers go jobless. And dollar for dollar, conservation investments create many more jobs than the construction and operation of highly capital-intensive electric power plants or synthetic fuels plants.

Improving national energy efficiency requires broad federal support. As described in Section II, numerous market imperfections and barriers inhibit the more efficient use of energy in this country. Unless these problems are overcome, the economy will continue to consume far more energy than is economically needed and Americans will pay the price for doing so through higher energy bills, higher rates of inflation and unemployment, reduced national security, and needless environmental degradation. Unfortunately, many of the programs needed to help the economy become more energy efficient are precisely those the Reagan Administration is eliminating.

Consumers cannot make economically justified energy investments if they do not have accurate information on the costs and benefits of investment alternatives. The Environmental Protection Agency's fuel-efficiency labeling program for cars and trucks exemplifies initiatives that can improve the market's workings by providing consumers with information on the relative efficiency of competing models. So too, appliance-labeling and building-labeling for energy performance deserve federal government's support, not opposition. Providing technical assistance for residential energy consumers through regulated utility involvement in the Residential Conservation Service program is another example of an information program that the country badly needs and that the Administration is drastically weakening. Providing consumers with accurate information fulfills a vital national need that the private sector cannot meet alone.

Federal efforts are also needed to overcome problems related to obtaining financing for conservation as well as for renewable energy measures. Many consumers simply do not have the capital to retrofit their homes, so they are stuck indefinitely with unnecessarily high energy bills. The same problem plagues many small commercial and industrial firms that don't have adequate cash flows to obtain loans or that find interest rates prohibitively high. But these problems are not intractable. Some electric utilities now have low- or no-interest loan programs for conservation and solar investments. These programs help consumers by providing the capital to reduce their energy bills and help utilities by cutting the need to build new generating capacity. Federal support of such programs is needed to eliminate the barriers to their widespread adoption. The federal Solar Energy and Energy Conservation Bank established by Congress would also address this problem by making low-interest loans available to low- and moderate-income households and small businesses. The bank deserves support. Instead, it is being eliminated.

Still other barriers that discourage cost-effective investments in energy efficiency need to be removed. Rented commercial and residential buildings face many barriers that inhibit cost-justified conservation and solar investments. The landlord-tenant problem, building codes, master-metering, some rent control laws, and old long-term leases that make it difficult to retrofit buildings are some of the entrenched barriers that need to be analyzed. If the federal government does not support analysis in these areas, it is unlikely to be carried out at all, and the nation's energy consumers will pay the price.

Federally supported research on conservation technology and related issues (such as the indoor air-quality problems arising from some conservation measures) is another important element of a federal energy policy. For reasons explained in Section II, private funding for both basic and applied conservation research is inadequate. Policy analysis, building design and operation, transportation system design, fundamental research to improve industrial processes and materials, and the prototype development and demonstration of new energy conservation technologies all warrant support.

The Administration has virtually eliminated funding for energy conservation research on grounds that industry will develop whatever the nation needs. But the interests of the marketplace and those of the nation cannot simply be equated. Industry operates within a relatively short time horizon and has as its goal the development of salable products that may or may not be important to national survival. The nation must necessarily take a longer perspective. Promoting global peace, supporting national economic growth, protecting the climate and our other natural resources, increasing national employment, and protecting those least able to help themselves—these important issues weigh significantly in the development of national policy but not in private decision-making. Even if the private sector can afford to ignore these factors in its research decisions, the federal government cannot.

Energy pricing remains perhaps the key to more efficient energy use. Indeed, the removal of price controls and the revision of state gas and electric rate structures to more accurately reflect the changing costs of new energy supplies is a policy that many environmental and public interest groups would support _if_ low- and middle-income Americans could be protected from unbearable price increases. If energy is priced significantly below its replacement value, consumers will tend to overuse fuels and underinvest in conservation measures that are not price-regulated.

The Reagan Administration's neglect of the needs of economically strapped Americans makes any form of additional price decontrol unacceptable at this time. By severely cutting the low-income weatherization program and dismantling the Solar Energy and Energy Conservation Bank, this Administration has made it clear it will not take even the smallest steps to protect those hit hardest by rising energy costs--the elderly, the recipients of public assistance, the working poor, and lower- and middle-income families who are already suffering the loss of food stamps, job training programs, college loans, and other programs designed to meet basic needs. However theoretically sound price decontrol and replacement cost pricing may be as long-term energy policies, adopting them now could intensify the harmful effects of program cuts on those individuals and geographic regions that are already bearing the brunt.

Other factors distort energy prices. Extraordinary tax breaks, development and commercialization funding, utilities' freedom from full financial responsibility for nuclear accidents, and the so-called "social costs" of failing to make dirty fuels environmentally acceptable--all of these subsidies encourage energy consumption and devalue energy efficiency in supplying basic energy services. All ought to be removed.

Laying the Foundations for a Solar Economy

Even as the economy grows more efficient, new energy sources will eventually be needed to replace dwindling domestic oil and gas supplies and to reduce the levels of imported oil. Fortunately, the United States has such resources. It is richly endowed with vast fossil, nuclear, and solar resources. In principle, any one of these three sources could ultimately meet most of our energy needs. Yet, each of these sources poses vastly different challenges and problems that must be taken into account in national energy planning. Their market prices alone do not reveal the long-range benefits and risks of each, and overwhelming scientific and political uncertainties make it impossible to fully translate risks into economic costs.

Increasing reliance on fossil or nuclear fuels has long-term climate, safety, and security ramifications that deserve close attention in the formulation of national policy. Coal constitutes about 90 percent of our remaining fossil fuels. If electric utilities and industry, its primary users, were to increase coal use substantially either by generating more electricity or producing synthetic oil and gas, serious environmental and social impacts would occur. The consequences would range from the industrial development of our western states--where most of our easily accessible coal resources are--to the enhanced build-up of carbon dioxide in the atmosphere.

The carbon dioxide problem poses long-term and essentially irreversible risks to the global climate.[79] Within a mattter of fifty years or so, continued fossil fuel burning could lead to an increase in the average global temperature of 3° C, resulting in changed patterns of rainfall and snow and ice cover, and eventually to a rise in sea levels if the West Antarctic ice sheet should disintegrate. World agriculture could be seriously disrupted and a significant rise in the oceans would flood many coastal cities around the world.

Prudence dictates, then, that coal burning be constrained so as to avoid increasing the risks of climate change. For this and other reasons, it would be a costly mistake to develop synthetic oil and gas from coal (or oil shale) on a wide scale. Doing so would commit us to enormous, long-term investments in synfuel plants and associated fuel-burning facilities--ranging from our

petroleum-powered transportation system to the oil- and gas-heating systems of
our buildings. These facilities could not possibly be replaced quickly enough
to stop climate changes once they have begun. If the carbon dioxide problem
is taken seriously, coal should be viewed only as a transitional fuel, one to
be used sparingly as we reduce our dependence on carbon-based energy sources.

Each of the nation's other two long-range energy options--nuclear energy
and renewable sources--could relieve us of the risks of climate changes,
though in vastly different ways and at very different costs. (Nuclear fusion
has yet to demonstrated technically feasible and is not considered here as an
available energy option.)

The problems posed by nuclear fission--high costs, unsolved safety
problems, plutonium proliferation, and radioactive waste management--have been
sketched in Section II of this report. The Reagan energy program does little
to deal constructively with these issues. A rational nuclear policy would
seek to improve the safety and fuel efficiency of existing nuclear plants,
solve the waste problem in a responsible manner, limit global commerce in
plutonium, and forestall the introduction of breeder reactors until the danger
of weapons proliferation they pose has been eliminated.

Whatever the source of the failure, the future of nuclear power is bleak
indeed, and its gradual phasing out appears likely. Counting on fission as an
important element of future energy supply would clearly be a mistake.

Renewable resources, our remaining option, are represented by many
different technologies. These include solar collectors and passive building
designs that can provide space heating, hot water, and steam for industry;
solar cells, wind turbines, and hydro dams that generate electricity; and
biofuels, such as wood and wastes.

Renewable energy sources pose neither the climate risks nor the security
and safety hazards of fossil and nuclear sources. And using solar energy

technologies entails far fewer environmental risks than conventional energy sources. Moreover, to the extent that their use reduces oil imports, they can help stabilize oil prices, improve the country's balance of payments, and enhance national security.

Renewable energy systems can provide stability and flexibility to the nation's energy supply and can be better matched to the end-uses for which energy is needed, thus reducing the nation's overall energy waste. (Almost half of the energy consumed in the United States is now directly wasted in energy conversion, transmission, or end-use losses.) Then too, renewable technologies are modular, so they can be brought into operation far more quickly than can large power plants or synthetic fuel plants.

Many renewable technologies are already cost-effective and are being used increasingly in a wide range of applications. Wood burning, the combustion of used paper and other solid wastes, low-head hydro dams, solar water-heating systems, passively designed buildings, and wind energy systems are all helping to meet an ever greater share of the nations's needs. Other solar technologies--most notably, photovoltaics--are developing rapidly and promise to be cost-effective in many settings by 1990.

Several major energy studies have concluded that by the turn of the century renewable energy sources could be meeting 20 to 30 percent of U.S. energy needs. Reaching this level, however, would require a concerted national effort aimed at improving the efficiency with which we perform tasks and use resources. It would also require an aggressvie program of introducing renewable energy sources. Such an effort can be realized only if the federal government acknowledges that conservation and solar technologies are viable alternatives to fossil and nuclear sources.

More specifically, the government must support research on technology development as well as systems integration. Because solar energy is intermittent, energy storage deserves special attention. An industrial economy powered by renewable resources will run largely from storage. Storage technologies are the key to making use of electricity from solar cells and wind turbines round the calendar and round the clock. Our transportation system--now powered almost entirely by liquid fossil fuels--poses a particulary difficult storage challenge. Hydrogen, derived from solar sources, and electric batteries both offer promising means for storing solar energy to power the vehicles of the future. If renewable resources are to meet a growing fraction of our energy needs, a major effort will be needed to develop and perfect low-cost, reliable storage technology.

There are other needs that the government is uniquely able to fulfill: providing consumers with reliable information on solar applications, making capital more accessible to those wishing to install solar systems, identifying and removing institutional barriers to the use of solar technologies, and confronting the problems of market distortion posed by energy subsidies.

*   *   *

The Administration and the Congress must recognize that the nation's energy future is not just a matter of chance, determined by uncontrollable market forces or unpredictable resource shortages. We are, in truth, masters of our own energy destiny. If we wish to make our economy more efficient and more reliant on renewable energy sources, the choice is ours. There are no physical, technical, or institutional barriers that we cannot overcome. What is needed most is a recognition by our national leaders that the important choices before us cannot be blindly left to the market place, and that by planning wisely we can safeguard the national interest while meeting our energy needs. We can create a safer and saner alternative than the radical, costly, dangerous, and inconsistent energy policy the Reagan Administration has proposed.

REFERENCES

1. Data from February 1982 News Release "Summary of Reagan FY 1983 Energy Budget Request" Subcommittee on Energy Conservation and Power, Committee on Energy and Commerce, U.S. House of Representatives, and personal communication, Andy Glassberg of the Subcommittee Staff, February 25, 1982.

2. "November National Poll," November 24, 1981, conducted by NBC News and The Associated Press, page 11.

3. "Nuclear Energy and the Public Under the Reagan Administration: Prospects for Ending the Stalemate," Eugene A. Rosa, et al., presented at the Annual Meeting of the American Association for the Advancement of Science, Washington, D.C., January 4, 1982, pages 12-13.

4. The economic problems being experienced by nuclear power plants are described in Power Plant Cost Escalation, Komanoff Energy Associates, New York, 1981, by Charles Komanoff; "Nuclear Fizzle?" by Michael Brody, Barrons's, August 24, 1981; "A Nuclear Fiasco Shakes the Bond Market," by Peter Bernstein, Fortune, February 22, 1982. Some of the generic technical problems related to steam generators and embrittlement at nuclear plants have been described in the New York Times: "Rusting Found In Key Section of 17 Reactors," 9/21/81; "Steel Turned Brittle by Radiation Called a Peril at 13 Nuclear Plants," 9/27/81; and "Nuclear Power's New Dilemma," October 4, 1981.

5. "The Impacts of Synthetic Fuels Development," David C. Masselli and Norman L. Dean, Jr., September, 1981, National Wildlife Federation.

6. The 1983 budget proposed for EPA represents a 39 percent reduction from 1981 while the agency's work load has essentially doubled.

7. See footnote 5. Also, "Synthetic Fuels and the Environment: An Environmental and Regulatory Impacts Analysis." June 1980, DOE/EV-0087.

8. Statement by the President, Office of the Press Secretary, The White House, October 8, 1981.

9. February 1982 News Release "Summary of Reagan FY 1983 Energy Budget Request" Subcommittee on Energy Conservation and Power, Committee on Energy and Commerce, U.S. House of Representatives.

10. Sixty-eight nuclear plants were cancelled between 1973 and 1980, see "Nuclear Fizzle?", footnote 4, supra. Thirteen additional plants have since been cancelled, see footnote 11.

11. Since the summer of 1981 the following 13 nuclear plants have been cancelled: Bailly, Callaway 2, Shearon Harris 3 and 4, Hope Creek 2, Pilgrim 2, Perkins 1, 2, and 3, Washington Public Power Supply System 3 and 4, and Black Fox 1 and 2.

12. The ads were summarized by NRC Commissiner Victor Gilinsky thus: "...this ad suggests that 33 plants can be made ready to operate in the next two years if only the regulators will stop dragging their feet. I've examined

those projects. On the basis of our experience with nuclear construction schedules, I would guess that no more than 20 of the 33 will actually be completed by then. I'm talking about construction delays and not licensing delays." Remarks of Victor Gilinsky, November 5, 1981 to the American Nuclear Society.

13. Letter from Nunzio J. Palladino, Chairman, U.S. Nuclear Regulatory Commission, to Rep. Tom Bevill, January 29, 1982, "NRC Monthly Status Report to Congress," pages 4, 5 and Table 1.

14. Remarks of Victor Gilinsky before the World Nuclear Fuel Market's International Conference on Nuclear Energy, October 27, 1981.

15. Remarks of Nunzio J. Palladino to Atomic Industrial Forum Annual Conference 1981, December 1, 1981.

16. "Analysis of Nuclear Power Economics," R. W. Hardie and G. R. Thayer, Los Alamos Scientific Laboratory, LA-8899-MS, June 1981, page 16.

17. "Barnwell Nuclear Fuel Plant to be Closed," Chemical and Engineering News, October 26, 1981, page 8.

18. "Weapons Builders Eye Civilian Reactor Fuel," Science 214, October 16, 1981, page 307.

19. Natural Resources Defense Council Press Release, "NRDC Challenges DOE Program to Use Commercial Nuclear Reactor Fuel to Make Atomic Bombs," July 24, 1981.

20. "Effort o Convert Reactor Waste to Military Use Arouses Alarm," New York Times, September 22, 1981.

21. Ibid.

22. See, e.g., "Proliferating Doubt" Wall St. Journal, Feb. 4, 1982; "Nuclear Cheating: Why the Experts Are Worried Over Safeguards," New York Times, December 22, 1981.

23. DOE Draft Supplemental Environmental Impact Statement, on the LMFBR Program, January, 1982.

24. Proposed Budget for the United States, Fiscal Year 1983.

25. Telegram from Edward Teller to U.S. Representative Claudine Schneider, May 11, 1981.

26. "Analysis of Nuclear Power Economics," R. W. Hardie and G. R. Thayer, Los Alamos Scientific Laboratory, LA-8899-MS, June 1981, page 18.

27. "Uranium, Electricity and Economics," Testimony before the Subcommittee on Energy Conservation and Power, of the House Committee on Energy and Commerce, Frank von Hippel, October 5, 1981, page 10.

28. "Atomic Apprenticeship," Editorial, Wall Street Journal, August 20, 1981.

29. "The Market Case Against the Clinch River Breeder Reactor," Rep. David Stockman, September 17, 1977.

30. Federal Energy R&D Priorities, R&D Panel of the Energy Research Advisory Board, November, 1981, page 27.

31. "Uranium, Electricity and Economics," Testimony before the Subcommittee on Energy Conservation and Power, of the House Committee on Energy and Commerce, Frank von Hippel, October 5, 1981, page 6.

32. Update, Nuclear Power Program Information and Data, October/December 1981, Office of Nuclear Reactor Programs, U.S. Department of Energy, page 95.

33. See, e.g., Komanoff, from footnote 4.

34. Statement of Theodore B. Taylor to Subcommittee on Oversight and Investigtions, Committee on Interior and Insular Affairs, October 23, 1981.

35. Ibid.

36. See, e.g. "Letting Nuclear Danger Spread," Jessica Tuchman Matthews, Washigton Post, December 2, 1981.

37. "Securing America's Energy Future, The National Energy Policy Plan," U.S. Department of Energy, July 1981, page 10.

38. Statement by the President, Office of the Press Secretary, The White House, October 8, 1981.

39. "Geologic Disposal of High-Level Radioactive Wastes--Earth-Science Perspectives," Geological Survey Circular 779, J.D. Bredehoeft, et al., 1978, page 12.

40. "Report to the President by the Interagency Review Group on Nuclear Waste Management," U.S. Department of Energy, TID-29442, March 1979, page 3.

41. The Lyons, Kansas debacle is described in The Atomic Establishment by H. Peter Metzger, (New York: Simon and Schuster, 1972), in Radidoactive Waste, by Ronnie D. Lipschutz, (Cambridge: Ballinger Publishing Co., 1980), and in "Radioactive Ashes in the Kansas Salt Cellar," John Lear, Saturday Review, February 19, 1972.

42. "Public Information Plan," U.S. Department of Energy Memorandum, September 24, 1981, from Eric. E. Anschutz to Shelby T. Brewer, Assistant Secretary for Nuclear Energy.

43. See footnote 2, supra, page 11.

44. See footnote 3, supra, page 19.

45. Ibid, page 10.

46. A clear, easily readable discussion of the Price Anderson Act and its effects on both the public andd the nuclear power industry can be found in

the booklet "Nuclear Insurance, Unavailable At Any Price," by Keiki Kehoe, 1980, The Environmental Policy Center, 317 Pennsylvania Ave., S.E., Washington, D.C. 20003, $2 postpaid.

47. In Fiscal Year 1981, prior to the first round of rescissions and deferrals requested by President Reagan, the federal energy conservation budget stood at $802 million at DOE (excluding Energy Impact Assistance) and $123 million at HUD (for the Solar Energy and Energy Conservation Bank.) See, e.g. Secretary's Annual Report to Congress, Vol. II, USDOE, January 1981.

48. Business Responses on Regulatory Burdens, An Initial Report Submitted to the Task Force on Regulatory Relief by the Department of Commerce, June, 1981, page 10.

49. House Resolution 243; Senate Resolution 232. Ninety-Seventh Congress.

50. See, e.g., Solar Energy Research Institute, A New Prosperity: Building a Sustainable Future, (Andover Mass.: Brick House Publishing, 1981) hereafter referred to as the "SERI Report"; John H. Gibbons and William U. Chandler, Energy--The Conservation Revolution (New York: Plenum Press, 1981); Marc H. Ross and Robert H. Williams, Our Energy: Regaining Control (New York: McGraw-Hill, 1981); Henry W. Kendall and Steven Nadis, Eds., Energy Strategies: Toward A Solar Future, (Cambridge, Mass.: Ballinger, 1980); The National Audubon Society, The Audubon Energy Plan, April, 1981; Hans H. Landsberg, Chairman, et al., Energy: The Next Twenty Years, Report by a study group sponsored by the Ford Foundation and administered by Resources for the Future (Cambridge, Mass.: Ballinger Publishing Company, 1979); National Research Council, Energy in Transition: 1985-2010, Final Report of the Committee on Nuclear and Alternative Energy Systems, Nsational Academy of Sciences (San Francisco: W.H. Freeman and Co., 1979); Robert Stobaugh and Daniel Yergin, Eds., Energy Future, Report of the Energy Project at the Harvard Business School (New York: Random House, 1979); Roger Sant et al., The Least Cost Energy Strategy, The Energy Productivity Center, Mellon Institutue (Pittsburgh: Carnegie-Mellon University Press, 1979); Domestic Policy Review Panel, The Domestic Policy Review of Solar Energy, A Response Memorandum to the President of the United States (U.S. Department of Energy, February 1979) TID-22834.

51. See, e.g. SERI Report, footnote 44, Table 2.2.

52. Ibid, Table 1.

53. U.S. Department of Energy, Monthly Energy Review, January, 1982, page 14.

54. Ibid.

55. Energy Conservation: The Road to New Growth in an Era of Uncertain Supply, A Report of the Energy Conservation Coalition, October 20, 1981, Table 4C, page 5.

56. See, e.g., Reducing U.S. Oil Vulnerability, U.S. Department of Energy, November 10, 1980, page 23: "At today's energy prices, economically justifiable retrofits to improve the energy efficiency of American homes would cost about $100 billion."

57. Office of Management and Budget, Fiscal Year 1981, Special Analysis G, page 226.

58. National Energy Conservation Policy Act (NECPA), Public Law 95-619, Title II, Part I.

59. Energy Policy and Conservation Act, Public Law 94-163, Title III, Part B.

60. Eric Hirst, "Improving Energy Efficiency: The Case for Government Action," ORNL, March 1981.

61. The energy conservation budget for research and development proposed for fiscal year 1983 is only $17.5 million. This compares to $182 million in fiscal year 1982 and $290 million in fiscal year 1981 (prior to rescissions.)

62. U.S. Department of Energy, Monthly Energy Review, January 1982, page 34.

63. See, e.g., Low-Income Energy Assistance: A Profile of Need and Policy Options, U.S. Department of Energy Fuel Oil Marketing Advisory Committee, July, 1980; Poor Plus Old Equals Cold, Grier Partnership, April, 1981.

64. According to OMB estimates contained in the Fiscal Year 1982 Budget, tax expenditures plus outlays for energy supply totaled $15 billion, while for fiscal year 1981, they totaled only $1.5 billion for energy conservation. See Special Analysis G, Table G-3.

65. Ibid.

66. Congressional Budget Office Report, September, 1981, "Tax Expenditures: Current Issues and Five Year Budget Projections for Fiscal Years 1982-1986."

67. The Economic Recovery Tax Act of 1981 included three new tax breaks for oil and gas concerns: a $2500 royalty credit for 1981, with a total exemption for 1982 and thereafter; a reduction in the tax on newly discovered oil; and an exemption from the windfall profit tax for independent-producer stripper-well oil. These three modifications alone will cost the federal treasury over $11 billion in lost revenues from 1982 to 1986, according to estimates of the Joint Committee on Taxation of the U.S. Congress, August 5, 1981.

68. These two polls are summarized in "The National Study of the Residential Solar Consumer: Decision Factors and Experiences—Preliminary Summary Report," Barbara Farhar Pilgrim et al., Solar Energy Research Institute, May, 1981.

69. SERI Report, see footnote 44, page 1.

70. Ibid.

71. Department of Energy, FY 1982 Congressional Budget Request, March 1981.

72. Statistical Abstract of the United States, 1980, Table 1615, page 937. The total number of occupied housing units is estimated to be 79 million.

73. Special Analysis G Basis, Office of Tax Analysis, Office of the Secretary of the Treasury, U.S. Treasury Department.

74. The proposed rules amending 10 CFR 456.315 appear in <u>Federal Register</u> <u>46</u> No. 218, Thursday, November 12, 1981.

75. Broyhill amendment to Omnibus Budget Reconciliation Act of 1981, June, 1981.

76. "Global Energy Futures and the Carbon Dioxide Problem," Council on Environmental Quality, January, 1981.

77. "Meeting the Challenge of the Times: An Austere Renewable Energy Budget," Solar Lobby, Solar Energy Industries Association, May, 1981, page 10.

78. U.S. Department of Energy, Monthly Energy Review, January 1982, page 14.

79. See, e.g., Footnote 76.

ALTERNATIVE BUDGET PROPOSALS

FOR THE ENVIRONMENT
FISCAL YEAR 1983

ENVIRONMENTAL POLICY CENTER
FRIENDS OF THE EARTH
IZAAK WALTON LEAGUE OF AMERICA
NATIONAL AUDUBON SOCIETY
NATIONAL PARKS & CONSERVATION ASSOCIATION
NATIONAL WILDLIFE FEDERATION
NATURAL RESOURCES DEFENSE COUNCIL
PRESERVATION ACTION
SIERRA CLUB
SOLAR LOBBY
THE WILDERNESS SOCIETY

MARCH 1, 1982

PREFACE

President Reagan's budget for 1983 would starve environmental protection. It does not need to. If wasteful, harmful subsidies in the energy, transportation, and natural resource areas are removed, and if special interest users of government services are made to pay their own way, there is plenty of room in our national budget for adequate protection of public health and the environment. The destruction of environmental programs in the President's budget is a policy choice, not a fiscal necessity.

The authors of this report are 11 conservation organizations representing over 5 million people. In our judgment, the Reagan Administration's cuts in spending for environmental protection and conservation of natural resources have gone much too far. Accordingly, on the spending side of the budget, we are recommending about $600 million more in outlays and $1.7 billion more in budget authority for FY 1983 than the Reagan Administration proposes. But on the revenue side, our proposals would bring in $9.1 billion more than the President's budget. We would accomplish this, not by raising the general level of taxation, but by closing tax loopholes, improving collection of royalties for resources on the public lands, and imposing user fees for government services in the resource and environment area.

Our recommendations would:

o   reduce the deficit by $8.5 billion;

o   restore an adequate, balanced program for protection of public health and the natural environment, and wise management of our nation's resources.

Our analysis covers major programs in energy, natural resources and public lands, transportation, and pollution control. We are most troubled by evidence that the Reagan Administration is turning its back on pollution control. For the second year in a row, the President's budget proposes deep cuts for the Environmental Protection Agency. The agency cannot take cuts of nearly 30 percent in two years (40 percent in real dollars), just when it must double its workload to deal with hazardous wastes and toxic chemicals in the environment. We believe the American people expect their government to protect them against future Love Canals. Of the $1.7 billion in additional spending authority our budget recommends above the Reagan budget, three-fourths is for the EPA.

In all the areas we reviewed, we found that the Reagan budget reorders national priorities away from conservation and protection of the environment toward support for a few resource extractive industries. We found a continued trend toward spending for economically dubious, environmentally damaging development at the expense of less costly, more benign alternatives.

For the second year, the Reagan budget would cut federal support for energy conservation and solar technologies to a vestige, while subsidizing white elephants of the nuclear power industry. Once again, the Reagan Administration proposes to construct the last 5 percent of the interstate highway system, at ballooning costs of millions of dollars per mile, while skimping on repair of existing highways and cutting support of energy-saving urban transit systems. In the area of natural resources, the Reagan budget chooses pork barrel water projects and subsidies to the timber industry over adequate protection of natural areas and wildlife habitat.

With some of the President's budget choices, we are in agreement. We support the Administration's proposals for user fees for government-built ports and waterways and we agree with the concept of requiring the nuclear power industry to pay waste management fees. Our proposals go much farther in this direction. In a time when government spending is coming under the closest scrutiny, it makes no sense to continue subsidies and tax breaks that do not achieve the intended goals, waste money, and do harm to the environment. If we make essential reforms on the revenue side, we can well afford the level of environmental protection that we really need.

ALTERNATIVE BUDGET PROPOSALS FOR THE ENVIRONMENT

Budget Functions	Change from President's Budget (in millions)	
	FY 1983 Authority	FY 1983 Outlays

EXPENDITURES

270 Energy

271 Energy Supply			
- Solar & Renewable R&D	+	200	+	80
- (DOE) Nuclear Programs	−	290	−	210
- Synthetic Fuels Corp.	−	40	−	40
272 Energy Conservation	+	650	+	290

300 Natural Resources & Environment

301 Water Resources Development	−	600	−	600
302 Conservation & Land Management	−	50	−	60
303 Recreation Resources			
- Land & Water Conservation Fund	+	330	+	220
- Other	+	320	+	230
304 Pollution Control & Abatement (EPA)	+	1,320	+	1,170

400 Transportation

401 Highways	−	1,800	−	1,350
402 Railroads	+	190	+	190
403 Mass Transit	+	1,500	+	680
Net Change in Expenditures	+	1,730	+	600

REVENUES

Royalties & User Fees

271 Fair Market Pricing of Uranium Enrichment Services	+ 525
271 Improved Oil & Gas Royalty Collection	+ 300
302 Grazing Fees	+ 100
304 Ocean Dumping Fee	+ 250
306 Royalties for Hard Rock Minerals	+2,000
401 Heavy Truck Highway User Fees	+1,300
802 Federal Parking Fees	+ 30
Subtotal - Royalties & User Fees	+4,505

Tax Expenditures

271 Expensing of Intangible Oil & Gas Drilling Costs	+3,500
271 Capital Gains Treatment of Royalties on Coal	+ 120
271 Industrial Energy Conservation Credit	− 180
302 Capital Gains Treatment of Timber	+ 300
306 Tax Exemptions for Nonfuel Minerals	+ 465
371 Personal Tax Deductions for Interest on 2nd & 3rd Homes	+ 400
Subtotal - Tax Expenditures	+4,605

Net Change in Revenues	+9,110

NET CHANGE IN DEFICIT	−8,510

FY 1983 ENERGY FUNCTION *

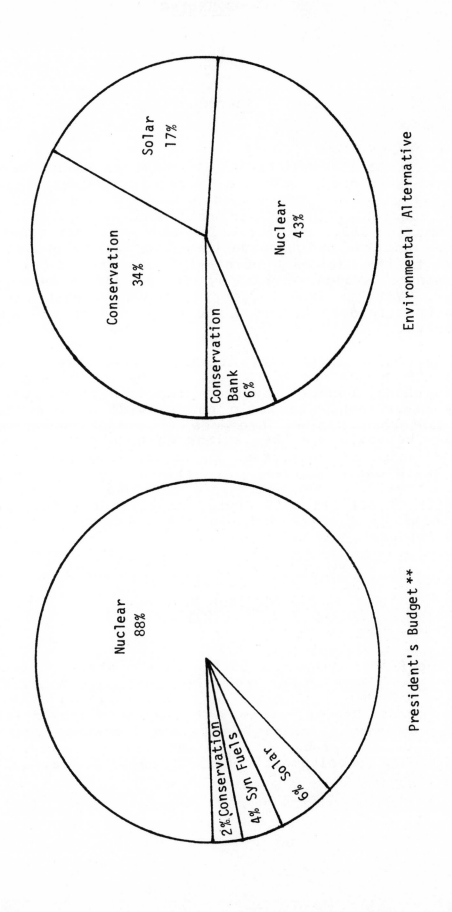

Nuclear
88%

2% Conservation
4% Syn Fuels

Solar
6%

President's Budget **

Solar
17%

Conservation
34%

Conservation
Bank
6%

Nuclear
43%

Environmental Alternative

*Percentages illustrate that portion of the overall Federal Budget
discussed in the text.

**0% earmarked in President's Budget for Conservation Bank

SPENDING

ENERGY
270

Introduction

Government subsidy of nuclear power is now in its fourth
decade. Some government analyses have estimated that the total
taxpayer subsidies, over the years, to nuclear energy are more
than $37 billion. The Reagan Administration wants to continue
these subsidies, providing more than $1 billion for nuclear
programs in 1983. But for solar energy, other renewable energy
sources and energy conservation, the Reagan budget cuts funds
almost to the vanishing point--to less than $100 million. The
President's avowed philosophy is to leave energy to market
forces. Yet his 1983 budget continues to wrap the padding of
taxpayer subsidies around white elephants of the nuclear power
industry.

Our budget sets very different priorities. In our judgment, the Reagan nuclear budget can be cut by almost $300 mil-
lion without touching necessary research in nuclear safety and
waste management. We would not provide a penny for wasteful
and dangerous nuclear projects that the Reagan budget supports. We would use the savings to help pay for necessary investments by the government in solar, renewable, and conservation energy alternatives. We believe that investment in these
alternatives will be repaid in future years many times over--in
security of our nation's energy supply; in safer, less polluting forms of energy; and, in the long run, in lower dollar
costs for energy as well.

Nuclear Programs
271

The Reagan budget gives the lion's share of federal energy
research and development money to the Liquid Metal Fast Breeder
Reactor (LMFBR). It would pour $253 million into the Clinch
River Breeder Reactor alone. The amount proposed for this outmoded, uneconomic, taxpayer-subsidized breeder reactor is more
than twice the proposed investment in all non-nuclear energy
research and development combined--coal, shale, solar, conservation, the works.

Our alternative budget would cut $293 million from the Administration's requested funding for nuclear fission for FY 1983. (Outlays for the year would be cut by $211 million.) Our budget would completely eliminate the Clinch River Breeder, the Advanced Isotope Separation program, and the $10 million line item for the Barnwell Nuclear Plant in South Carolina.

The Clinch River Breeder, a demonstration LMFBR, has been plagued by unprecedented cost overruns and technical management problems. Its projected total cost has now risen from the originally authorized level of $700 million to above $3.5 billion. The taxpayers will be expected to foot at least 90 percent of this skyrocketing bill.

Construction on the Clinch River Breeder has not yet begun. Utility analysts estimate that breeder technology will not be price competitive with light water reactors (currently the dominant type of nuclear power reactor in the United States) until the price of uranium rises above $165 per pound. The price is now about $25 per pound. Thus, commercialization of the breeder is uncertain for the foreseeable future. The Clinch River Breeder is both premature and obsolescent—possibly a unique combination. It represents a form of breeder technology already demonstrated in France. While this fact does not mitigate its economic problems, it does considerably reduce its research value. The Clinch River Breeder should be terminated.

The Advanced Isotope Separation program includes as a component the Plutonium Laser Isotope Separation program which is being developed at the Lawrence Livermore Laboratory. (This program is also partly funded through the DOE/ERTA Defense budget.) The program forms the research base for the dangerous proposal to use spent fuel from the nation's 75 commercial nuclear power plants as a feedstock for the production of nuclear weapons. If the program were to succeed, it would raise the potential for proliferation of nuclear weapons to nightmarish proportions. It would forever break the thin line between the "peaceful" and warlike uses of nuclear power. The program should be terminated.

Finally, our alternative budget recommends cutting off federal life-support activities for the moribund Barnwell Nuclear Plant. Barnwell is another in the long line of failed private reprocessing ventures. Its technical and economic problems are so severe that its parent company, Allied General Nuclear Services, has already begun to write it off its books. We taxpayers should write it off our books, too.

It should be noted that the Reagan budget assumes passage of a law requiring that commercial nuclear reactor operators contribute to a waste management fund, bringing in about $300 million for FY 1983. We strongly support the idea of a users' fee for nuclear waste management, provided it recovers all the costs on a businesslike basis, rather than hiding a continuing subsidy with a figleaf.

Solar and Renewable Energy Research and Development
271

The Reagan budget would slash funds for solar and renewable energy R&D to less than 15 percent of last year's level--this after funds had already been cut last year to less than half the FY 1981 level. The Reagan budget would leave only $73 million in budget authority for solar and renewable energy R&D. Our alternative budget would provide $275 million, which is equal to the amount Congress approved last year. Solar and renewable energy are too important in the mix of energy sources for our nation's future to be neglected.

The Reagan budget's wholesale abandonment of renewable energy R&D would undercut years of federally supported work which is just now beginning to bear fruit. Many of these technologies are still in the development stage, too far from commercialization to make it on their own without government support. For example, federally-supported research on photovoltaic cells (which convert solar energy directly into electricity) has brought the cost down from $250,000 per kilowatt-hour to $10. The cost needs to drop still further for commercial feasibility. With government support for R&D drying up under the Reagan budget, this development could be long delayed.

While our government proposes to withdraw support from solar and renewable R&D, other countries--notably France, Germany and Japan--are increasing theirs. They are aggressively pursuing foreign markets, one of which is the United States.

The Environmental Alternative budget would support development of active and passive solar heating and cooling, photovoltaics, solar thermal energy, wind power, ocean thermal energy, alcohol fuels, and biomass. It would provide R&D support in such projects as:

o   high performance materials for photovoltaic
     cells, thermal storage, and glazing surfaces;

o   advanced plant species for fuel and chemical
     feedstocks;

o   large and small scale wind energy technolo-
     gies;

o   resource assessments for wind, solar and
     biomass; and

o   data collection and information dissemina-
     tion on renewable energy technologies.

Synthetic Fuels Program
271

The Energy Security Reserve was created in 1980 to subsidize the commercialization of synthetic fuels. In FY 1981,
$400 million of ESR funds were committed in price guarantees,
and $1.2 billion in loan guarantees. Two billion dollars ($2
billion) in loan guarantees have already been obligated in FY
82, and additional price and loan guarantees are projected to
be $4.5 billion in FY 1982, and $8 billion in FY 1983.

For FY 1983, the direct, on-budget expenses of the
Synthetic Fuels Corporation will be $36 million. This expense
is paltry, however, compared to the obligations the Corporation
is undertaking. If the synthetic fuels projects it is under-
writing do not prove cost competitive, the government may have
to lay out billions of dollars to cover the guarantees by the
late 1980s and 1990s. This outcome is unfortunately likely,
considering the present stabilization of oil prices and soaring
costs for synthetic fuel projects. Even if oil prices rise,
synfuels will face increased competition from greater energy
conservation and from other energy technologies that are dropping in cost and improving in performance. As one energy anal-
yst said: "Unless you believe in high petroleum demand growth
at high prices, synthetic fuels are never going to happen."

At a time when budget-cutting is reducing many social and environmental programs, it is totally inappropriate for the government to subsidize commercial investments by the energy industry, especially ones which are loaded with poorly understood environmental dangers. If investment in synfuels as a substitute for petroleum were really a sound investment, ample private investment funds should be available. Decontrol of oil, as the Congressional Budget Office noted, "has provided the energy industry with both the capital and the motivation to develop alternative sources for liquid fuels."

Our alternative budget recommends abolition of the Synthetic Fuels Corporation. The immediate on-budget saving for FY 1983 will be $36 million. In later years, the saving will in all likelihood be many billions of taxpayers' dollars.

Energy Conservation Programs
272

The Reagan budget would cut energy conservation programs to $22 million, 94 percent below the $386 million appropriated for FY 1982. The cut since President Reagan took office would be 97 percent. The President's budget abandons federal leadership or concern for eliminating barriers to the efficient use of energy.

The Reagan budget cuts reflect the erroneous beliefs that the energy crisis is over and that higher prices will encourage all the conservation that is needed. In fact, we are as dependent on foreign oil today as we were in 1973. Worse, soaring energy prices have doubled the percentage of GNP that now must go to energy. Annual retail expenditures for energy have topped $400 billion--nearly $2000 per capita!

The Reagan budget cuts do not recognize the imperfections of the marketplace that have left undone at least $100 billion worth of cost-effective energy efficiency investments. Without information programs, consumers may not be aware of the best ways to save energy and money. Without research programs, energy conserving equipment may not reach the marketplace. Without state and local involvement, the energy conservation problems of low income families will not be met.

The Administration's proposal would wipe out the Low-Income Weatherization program, the Schools and Hospitals program, the State Energy Conservation programs, State Emergency Planning funds, the Energy Extension Service, minimum energy performance standards for new appliances, the Residential Conservation Audit Service, and most energy efficiency research programs--notably, all industrial and almost all buildings and transportation energy conservation research. In short, most of the bipartisan energy conservation initiatives of the last three Administrations would be eliminated.

The DOE energy conservation budget we propose--$575 million for FY 1983--is at the level authorized by Congress for FY 1982 in the Omnibus Reconciliation Act of 1981. It constrains spending while still allowing for the continuation of essential and highly successful programs. It helps to remove barriers to energy efficiency in the marketplace. And it permits the United States to maintain a leadership role in developing energy-efficient technologies.

Solar and Energy Conservation Bank
272

This program, authorized by Congress in 1981, has been repeatedly delayed by the Administration's attempts to kill it in spite of clear Congressional intent. Congress appropriated start-up funds of $23 million for FY 1982, but the Reagan Administration has refused to assign any staff or resources to implement the statutory mandate, and is proposing to rescind the appropriated funds. The Reagan budget provides no funding for FY 1983.

The Bank is designed to enable local lenders to offer below-market interest rates on investments in energy efficiency and renewable energy, particularly for middle and low income Americans who otherwise could not make these investments. Delaying or wiping out the program is especially harmful during the current period of high interest rates.

Our alternative budget proposes $100 million in budget authority for the program, enabling the Bank to advance from its start-up phase. At the level we propose, the Bank's program could directly reach 85,000 homes in FY 1983, reducing energy use in each home by 25 percent and saving the equivalent of an estimated 9 million barrels of oil over the lifetime of the investments.

FY 1983 NATURAL RESOURCES AND ENVIRONMENT *

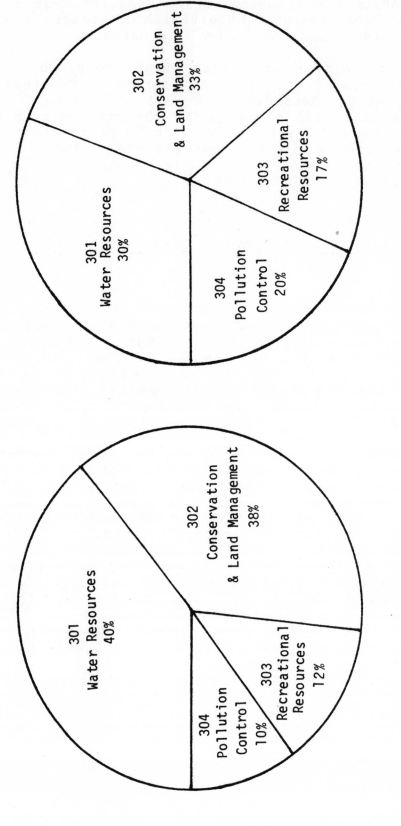

301
Water Resources
40%

302
Conservation
& Land Management
38%

304
Pollution
Control
10%

303
Recreational
Resources
12%

President's Budget

302
Conservation
& Land Management
33%

301
Water Resources
30%

303
Recreational
Resources
17%

304
Pollution
Control
20%

Environmental Alternative

*Percentages illustrate that portion of the overall Federal Budget discussed in the text.

NATURAL RESOURCES AND ENVIRONMENT
300

Introduction

In President Reagan's budget, development and commercial exploitation of natural resources is amply supported, while conservation programs are cut or zeroed out. The Reagan budget proposes continued high spending for water projects, with little regard for whether the projects are economically sensible and environmentally sound. It provides more money for timber sales and extraction of oil and gas on public lands, and much less for parks, wildlife, and coastal zone protection.

The Environmental Alternative budget would restore more balance. Our total spending figure is roughly the same as that of the Reagan budget. We see plenty of opportunity to save $600 million in a water projects budget of nearly $4 billion by getting rid of wasteful, environmentally harmful projects and postponing marginal ones. Our budget also cuts out $150 million in subsidies to the timber industry.

We propose using the savings to care for the nation's parks and natural areas, beaches and estuaries, watersheds and wildlife. Many of these resources have little immediate commercial value, in the usual sense. Often overlooked is the economic value they contribute in sustaining fisheries, public water supplies, sport hunting and fishing, and many other kinds of recreation. They also contribute intangibles--scenic beauty, undisturbed nature--which have priceless, enduring value for generations to come.

Water Resources Development
301

The Reagan budget would reduce overall spending for water resource projects slightly from last year's level. However, for the Bureau of Reclamation, the dam-building agency in the Department of the Interior, the Administration is requesting an increase of $180 million or more than 20 percent, despite the extensive record which documents the Bureau's financial mismanagement and the unsound economics it uses to justify its projects. The Bureau operates exclusively in the 17 western states, with a heavy emphasis on irrigated agriculture. The Reagan budget reduces the Army Corps of Engineers program by

6 percent to about $2.7 billion.* The Corps operates a multipurpose water resource development program nationwide.

The Reagan budget would also sharply reduce the Soil Conservation Service's small watershed program. We agree with this reduction. The program has dammed or channelized hundreds of small streams over the last 25 years in an ineffective, and environmentally damaging, attempt at rural flood control. The interagency Water Resources Council is eliminated in the Reagan budget. This small agency has done the valuable work of issuing standards for rational planning and evaluation of water resource projects.

Many federal water projects now under construction are economically inefficient as well as environmentally destructive. In recent years such projects as the Tennessee-Tombigbee Waterway, the Garrison Diversion, and the Stonewall Jackson Dam have been questioned by Congressional committees and challenged on the floor of House and Senate. The Reagan budget for FY 1983 provides about $900 million for these and other unsound projects.

It may not be politically expedient to remove all unsound projects from the water resource agenda--although we note that President Reagan has confounded past political experience in managing budget cuts in other areas. In any case, there is plenty of room for shrinkage in the water resource budget. Also, many marginal projects can be postponed, scaled down, or eliminated, providing funds that may be reallocated to speed up meritorious projects, or to plan sound projects.

Sensible cuts in funds for water resource projects could yield net savings of $600 million in budget authority and outlays for FY 1983.

U.S. Forest Service Activities
302

The Reagan Administration proposes a budget of $2.1 billion for the Forest Service, about the same amount as Congress

---

*The Reagan budget shows spending by the Corps of $2.2 billion, which includes offsetting receipts of $525 million from port and waterway user fees proposed by the Administration. We strongly support this proposal; see the Revenues section of this report.

appropriated in FY 1982. But the similar totals mask significant shifts in spending: The Reagan budget proposes sharp increases for managing minerals and timber production, including bigger subsidies for the timber industry, while cutting basic support for other essential multiple use activities--protection of soil and water, fish and wildlife, and recreation.

While the Reagan Administration says it wants to reduce government subsidies that interfere with the marketplace, the $665 million it has requested for a much expanded timber sales program includes about $150 million in subsidies to the timber industry. The budget provides for sales of 12.3 billion board feet in 1983, up from the 11 billion board feet provided for in 1982 appropriations.

The Forest Service acknowledges that 22 percent of the volume of National Forest timber sold fails to cover costs. If the Forest Service eliminates "sales-below-costs" that provide hidden subsidies to the industry, the timber sale level would probably be about 9.6 billion board feet. Consequent savings in sales administration, other management costs, and road construction would reduce the Forest Service budget by $150 million.

Cutting out subsidies and reducing timber sales makes good policy as well as good fiscal sense. The proposed increases in sales are not necessary. The amount of timber that the Forest Service has already sold but the buyers have not yet cut is a record high 36 billion board feet--more than three years worth of average timber sales from the national forests. In addition, the Forest Service has recently allowed time extensions for cutting under current timber sale contracts, further swelling the backlog. If the Forest Service adjusts its timber sales to realistic market conditions, sales of 9.6 billion board feet in FY 1983 seem more than sufficient.

Moreover, Federal timber sales do not necessarily increase total national supplies. In fact, federal sales-below-cost may discourage investments and production for profit on private lands. They may substitute for private timber that would otherwise be cut. Congress has mandated that our national forests be managed for multiple uses and values--for example, protection of wilderness, watersheds, and wildlife, including threatened and endangered species, as well as for timber production. Thus public policy should encourage supplies from the private, non-industrial timber lands, which comprise 58 percent of the nation's commercial timber lands, rather than discouraging it by providing subsidized timber from national forests.

Besides the distortions caused by subsidies, the Forest Service budget is inequitably distributed among the multiple uses which the law requires the Forest Service to provide. The 1980 Program for the Resources Planning Act (RPA) (which was ratified by a bipartisan vote in the 96th Congress) sets forth a professional assessment of how the Forest Service should allocate its spending to provide for balanced multiple use in our national forests. The Administration's 1983 budget ignores this professional assessment. Instead, it skews the budget toward commodity production (timber and minerals) at the expense of non-commodity uses (wildlife, recreation, soil and water protection). For example, the Administration funds timber production at about 75 percent of the 1983 RPA goal, and trail construction at a mere 24 percent of the 1983 RPA Program. We propose that of the $150 million saved by eliminating deficit timber sales, $50 million be distributed to those forest uses which receive the least support in comparison to the RPA professional assessment.

Bureau of Land Management Activities
302

The Reagan Administration's budget continues the trend, begun last year, of accelerating resource development at the expense of planning, analysis, and environmental protection. Extraction of nonrenewable resources such as oil, gas, coal and other minerals takes precedence over the management of renewable resources such as forage, water, soil, wildlife, and air. The FY 1983 budget cuts $10.8 million from renewable resource management while adding $7.6 million to the minerals program to accelerate leasing and permitting.

The proposed increase in mineral leasing will put added burdens on the Bureau's planning and analysis capability. Yet, the planning budget for 1983 was cut $1.5 million or 17 percent from the 1982 level. This, combined with the large cut in 1982 and the effects of inflation, has reduced BLM's planning capability by more than 50 percent in only two years.

The weakening of planning capability by 50% will result in ad hoc decision-making. It will interfere with the agency's ability to resolve questions about the effects on resources and the environment of accelerated minerals development. The Federal Land Policy and Management Act mandates comprehensive land use planning as the basis for land use management decisions. With the cuts in planning proposed by the Reagan budget, these plans will not be completed until the next century. The failure to carry out required planning could invite lawsuits and thus delay even well-conceived energy and minerals development.

The Environmental Alternative budget would increase BLM's budget by $5.2 million for planning and $7.8 million for renewable resources management. At the same time, it proposes $8.5 million less than the President's budget for energy and minerals management, for a better balance between extractive and planning areas of the budget. Our budget calls for a net increase of $4.5 million in BLM's spending. We believe this small increase will result in better, faster, and more defensible land use decisions for BLM lands. To continue along the course charted by the FY 1982 budget and the Reagan budget for 1983 would mean exploitation of public land resources without enough consideration of environmental impacts and conflicts with renewable resource management goals.

Office of Surface Mining
302

The FY 1983 Reagan budget for the Office of Surface Mining represents a significant retreat from the previous Administration's commitment to diligent enforcment of the Federal Surface Mining Control and Reclamation Act of 1977. The Reagan Administration is attempting to rationalize budget cuts in the program by pointing to its policy of reducing federal involvement as a necessary result of the shift of regulatory primacy from the Office of Surface Mining to the States. This shift in regulatory responsibility ought not occur without adequate funding for OSM to maintain critical federal oversight responsibilities mandated by the strip mining law and for technical assistance to those states assuming the entire program, including the regulation of mining activities on federal lands. These two important functions are destined for significant cuts in the Reagan budget.

The OSM requests nearly the same level of funding for FY 1983 as for FY 1982. However, it plans to significantly reallocate its expenditures to implement its delegation of authority to the States. The plan entails the shift of federal dollars to the States to compensate their administrative costs at the expense of its mandatory oversight and technical assistance responsibilities. In effect, its field enforcement and technical analysis capabilities will be seriously eroded in contradiction to the federal law. Additionally, OSM intends to achieve a reduction of the present field inspection staff from 145 to 69 employees. However, last year the Congress appropriated monies sufficient to maintain OSM's inspection force, thereby intending the fulfillment of statutory obligations. In spite of this, OSM has failed in FY 1982 to fulfill its enforcement tasks, citing insufficient funding as a reason.

We recommend that OSM's FY 1983 budget receive the same level of funding as its FY 1982 budget. However, the allocation of this budget should be based upon its regulatory, inspection, and enforcement responsibilities. OSM should be required to spend the money appropriated to hire adequate technical and inspection personnel and support staff to meet its legislative mandates. Once all the states have approved regulatory programs in place, we recommend the OSM maintain at least 100 inspectors to fulfill its oversight responsibilities. Without these staffing levels, the government will be unable to verify compliance on the part of the states, and to respond to environmental emergencies and other citizen requests.

Coastal Zone Management
302

Coastal Zone Management, a federal-state partnership to ensure rational planning for our dwindling coastal resources, will end in FY 1982 unless the Congress moves to restore funding for this important program. Presently 26 states and territories have federally approved coastal plans and are implementing those plans with the help of federal funding at a modest level, with an 80-20 federal-state match. Termination of funding for this program could not come at a worse time for the states, which are facing a massive speedup in offshore drilling along their coasts. This pressure, plus the move toward increased port expansion to accommodate coal exports, indicates a greater need for careful coastal planning than ever before.

Under the Coastal Zone Management Program, states have received small planning grants to inventory their coastal resources, designate critical areas off-limits to development, and plan for orderly development in other appropriate areas. Through coastal planning, states are able to safeguard important local economies such as commercial and recreational fishing and coastal tourism. Furthermore, successful coastal zone management enables the states to provide the kind of predictability for development planning that energy-related industries are seeking.

Targeted for elimination by the Reagan Administration in FY 1982, CZM was rescued by the Congress, which deferred $33 million in FY 1981 Coastal Energy Impact funds to guarantee CZM funding through 1982. Our alternative budget proposes $40 million in state grants for FY 1983, including grants for two new states, New York and New Hampshire, plus $10 million for managing marine and estuarine sanctuaries programs and running the national Coastal Zone Management Office.

Fish and Wildlife Service Activities
303

The Reagan budget proposes almost as much funding for the Fish and Wildlife Service in FY 1983 as in FY 1982--but the FY 1982 budget had been cut substantially from the year before. Perhaps more important, environmental analysis and protection are suffering disproportionately. Funds have been slashed from habitat preservation, endangered species protection, fisheries research and protection, and acquisition of land. Programs which gain in the Reagan FY 1983 budget are in "operation and maintenance," a large, varied category which includes refurbishing of facilities.

An important example of the proposed cuts in conservation activities is the endangered species program. The Reagan budget for FY 1983 would cut the program back 25 percent from the FY 1981 level, reducing spending from $22 million to $16.5 million. Funded at a spare level to begin with, in relation to its critically important duties, the endangered species program would suffer grievously from cuts that eliminate all state grants ($4 million), cut $1 million from enforcement, and cut another $1 million from listing of species and recovery measures. We recommend restoring endangered species activities to the FY 1981 level.

Another victim of the Reagan budget is the minerals program of the Office of Biological Services, which would be abolished entirely. This program assesses the impacts on fish and wildlife of oil shale, tar sands, and geothermal energy development. Other environmental assessment activity, including study of the effects of the coal leasing program, has also been proposed for cuts.

A particularly damaging loss is in programs that assist states. For example, for the second year, the Administration has proposed eliminating the Cooperative Wildlife and Fisheries Unit Program under which the FWS cooperates on research with state universities and state wildlife agencies. Last year Congress reinstated this $4.4 million program. The National Wildlife Health Laboratory is another example. This diagnostic and research laboratory is very useful to state wildlife management because of its unduplicated work on diseases of migratory birds. The Reagan budget has marked the lab for elimination in FY 1983, as it did in FY 1982.

Our alternative budget proposes an additional $16 million for research, development permit review and assessment, endangered species protection, and work on fishery resources. We support the Reagan budget's proposal for a 50 percent increase for the National Wetlands Inventory. We also recommend that the Congress reauthorize the Migratory Bird Conservation Account, which is now due to expire at the end of FY 1983. Under this program, the FWS can borrow from the Treasury for the purchase of critical wetlands, repaying the loan from the proceeds from future duck stamp sales.

Land and Water Conservation Fund
303

For the second year, the Reagan Administration has proposed slashing appropriations for the Land and Water Conservation Fund (LWCF), to extremely low levels. The Fund, created by Congress in 1965, is the primary source of money for acquiring or completing parks, wildlife refuges, and other recreation areas. It is also an important source of funds for buying and developing state and local parks. Offshore oil and gas revenues provide most of the money for the Fund. These revenues, according to Administration estimates, will reach $18 billion annually by 1983.

Currently, the authorized level for the Fund is $900 million annually. Actual appropriations in the last five fiscal years have averaged about $500 million. In FY 1982, the Reagan Administration proposed a level of $39.6 million for the LWCF. All of this small amount was to be used by federal agencies for two purposes: paying claims won in court by landowners for sale of their property and program administration. No funding was proposed for the state matching grant program. In most years, Congress has allocated about 40 percent of appropriations to federal acquisition (the minimum allowed by the law); the rest has gone to state governments in 50-50 matching grants.

Congress found the $39.6 million proposed in the FY 1982 Reagan budget entirely inadequate. This amount would not have been enough even for a bare minimum of land purchases already authorized by Congress, or for the exercise of options to purchase lands that are about to expire. Congress appropriated $149.2 million for FY 1982, and rejected two-thirds of the Administration's proposed recission of FY 1981 funding.

For FY 1983, the Administration has again recommended a totally inadequate amount--$69.4 million, to be available to the federal agencies only, and to be used almost exclusively to pay for pending or anticipated court awards to landowners. Funding at this low level would mean the permanent loss of thousands of acres of parks, refuges, and other areas authorized for purchase by Congress, as irreversible development destroys natural areas and wildlife habitat.

Funds are needed to protect lands in approximately 100 different federal areas in all parts of the country. Some of the projects requiring funding in FY 1983 are the Appalachian National Scenic Trail, Lake Tahoe, Olympic National Park, Tensas River National Wildlife Refuge, and the Franklin D. Roosevelt National Historical Site at Hyde Park. Funds are also needed to preserve critical habitat for several threatened or endangered species, including the American crocodile, bald eagle and peregrine falcon.

Termination of the state matching grant portion of the Land and Water Conservation Fund, as the Reagan budget proposes, would be very damaging. The program has been highly effective in preserving and developing outdoor recreation areas for public use in all states and territories. It is a good example of what President Reagan has termed the "new federalism." The 50 percent state match required by the program effectively doubles the federal grants, partly through the use of private donations. In the fifteen years of the program's existence more than 2 million acres have been protected; nearly 20,000 projects to develop state and local outdoor recreation facilities have been funded. Although Congress provided no funding for the state matching grant portion of the LWCF in FY 1982, it made clear that the lack of funding was a one-year moratorium and that it expected funding to be resumed in FY 1983.

We are recommending $400 million in FY 1983 for the LWCF. This level, an increase over the FY 1982 appropriation, is still 20 percent below the average appropriation for the past five years.

National Park Service Operations
303

The Reagan Administration has stressed the need to be good stewards of the National Park System. In attempting to accomplish this, the Administration has focused its attention on repairing and rehabilitating structures and facilities in the National Park System. Good stewardship, however, goes far beyond rehabilitating roads and buildings. Above all, it includes the preservation of the natural and cultural resources which the National Park System was established to protect.

Recent hearings on the state of the National Park System in the House Subcommittee on Public Lands and National Parks revealed widespread and pervasive threats throughout the System to the very resources that the parks were designed to protect. Among the problems discussed at the hearings were air and water pollution, urban encroachment on park borders, and development and clearcutting actually occurring within park boundaries. The Park Service's "State of the Parks" report of 1980 found that:

No parks of the System are immune to external and internal threats, and these threats are causing significant and demonstrable damage. There is no question but that these threats will continue to degrade and destroy irreplaceable park resources until such time as mitigation measures are implemented.

The Reagan budget for FY 1983 does not recommend enough funding for preservation of the all-important natural and historic resources. Extra funding for this purpose would allow the Service to address specific critical problems of various parks, as identified in the "State of the Parks" report. To solve these problems, and for more general purposes, the Park Service needs new resource management staff and an augmented science and research program.

Our alternative budget does not propose any increase in the overall budget for the National Park Service's operations. Instead, we recommend that approximately 15 percent of the agency's construction budget be used for natural and cultural resource protection.

Urban Parks Recovery Program
303

The Congressionally mandated National Urban Recreation Study, released in early 1978, revealed a tremendous need, nationwide, to rehabilitate existing recreational areas and facilities, especially in the more distressed communities. In recognition of this need, Congress enacted the Urban Parks and Recreation Recovery Program in late 1978 with an authorized spending level of $150 million a year for fiscal years 1979-82, and $125 million in FY 1983. To date, the federal government has awarded approximately 494 grants to communities, worth $124 million, under the program. This is the only national program designed specifically to meet major recreational problems in the neediest communities, especially the older central cities.

The Reagan budget for FY 1983 attempts to terminate this program, as did the FY 1982 budget. In FY 1982, Congress appropriated $7.7 million. For FY 1983, our alternative budget recommends $20 million.

Youth Conservation Employment
303

Youth Conservation workers have a proven record of accomplishing needed projects at low cost. In the National Park System, for example, the youth workers have done approximately $1.20 worth of work for every dollar of federal expenditure. Under the Reagan Administration, youth conservation employment programs have been virtually eliminated. The Administration's FY 1983 budget recommends zero funding.

Legislation introduced in the Congress would establish a new and more effective youth conservation employment program at a time of high and probably increasing unemployment. Funding for the program would come in part from Outer Continental Shelf revenues. By providing funding in this manner, revenues from a nonrenewable resource will be reinvested in our youth and our public lands.

In light of the high unemployment rates, especially among disadvantaged youth, and the need to improve the resources found on public lands, we believe that a case could easily be made for an appropriation in excess of $500 million. However, because of other pressing budget priorities, our alternative budget recommends $250 million to begin a much needed but minimal program. If unemployment worsens, a larger program would be needed.

If new legislation for Youth Conservation employment does not pass in time to receive FY 1983 appropriations, then we recommend that the $250 million be appropriated to the Departments of Interior and Agriculture to hire youth workers for the federal land management agencies in FY 1983.

National Historic Preservation Fund
303

The Reagan budget recommends zero funding for the National Historic Preservation Fund for FY 1983. This program, authorized in 1966, has not only carried out federal responsibilities for the National Register of Historic Places, but has provided grants to the states for related activities. It has also given matching grants to the National Trust for Historic Preservation, which fosters investment in preservation by the private sector. In FY 1982 Congress appropriated $25.4 million to carry out all these activities.

Both the state programs and the federal contribution to the Trust would be eliminated in the Reagan budget. Whatever functions remain would be carried out by the National Park Service. State activities, under federal matching grants, have included: preparing nominations to the National Register, certifying structures and rehabilitations for use of tax incentives, and reviewing federally-funded projects for their impact on historic resources. All these activities are mandated by federal law.

The state program is economical for the federal government, because the states match federal dollars. According to a report prepared by the Department of the Interior, it will cost the federal government more, both in dollars and in staff, to carry out the program itself. The states have been effective in promoting private investment for the rehabilitation of historic properties in towns and cities throughout the nation. And the state program is consistent with President Reagan's espousal of the new federalism.

Likewise, the activities of the National Trust for Historic Preservation have been effective. Chartered by Congress in 1949, the Trust preserves and operates several nationally significant historic properties. In addition, it stimulates interest and investment by the private sector in preservation, including revitalization of small town business districts and minority and low-income neighborhoods. The Historic Preservation Fund has provided about 40 percent of the budget for the Trust, with contributions ranging from $5.4 million in FY 1979 to $4.4 million in FY 1982.

Our alternative budget recommends the continuation of the Historic Preservation Fund, with an appropriation of $30 million for FY 1983.

Pollution Control and Abatement
304

EPA Operating Budget. The funding proposed for pollution control in the Reagan budget for FY 1983 is much too low. It reduces funds for the Environmental Protection Agency 29 percent from 1981 levels (39 percent in inflation-adjusted

dollars) just when the agency's work load is doubling. At the
level of funding proposed, EPA simply cannot do the work
Congress has given it to do, and provide the protection the
American public expects. The Reagan budget would destroy the
nation's environmental safety net.

The budget for EPA contradicts the Reagan Administration's
own statements on agency redirection. While the Administration
asserts that regulation should be based on "good science," it
cuts the research and development program 27 percent. While it
claims that states should accept more responsibility for pollution control, it cuts state grants by 20 percent. While it
highlights the war on toxics as a top program priority, it proposes substantial cuts in all six agency programs that attempt
to control the production, use, and disposal of toxic chemicals
(pesticides, toxic substances, air, water, hazardous wastes and
hazardous waste clean-up operations).

EPA's total operating budget was $1.35 billion in FY 1981.
The Reagan budget proposal is for $961 million in FY 1983.
This, at a time when the agency is struggling to develop new
programs to (1) research the effect of toxics on human health,
(2) remove existing toxics from air and water, (3) safely dispose of over 42 million tons of hazardous wastes each year, (4)
clean up over 30,000 abandoned toxic dumps scattered throughout
the country, and (5) prevent installed air and water pollution
control equipment from falling into disrepair and disuse.

Clearly, these new tasks--all of which EPA has been directed to undertake by Congress--cannot be effectively addressed within a budget that has suffered such disproportionate
cuts. The Environmental Alternative budget recommends $2.178
billion for EPA in 1983, a 36 percent increase over the FY 1981
level, and a more than 100 percent increase over the Reagan
budget proposal. This increase is fully justified if EPA is to
carry out its duty, required by law, to control the toxic substances that threatens the health of American citizens and endanger the natural environment.

Funds for EPA's Research and Development should be substantially increased to adequately research the health effects of
pollutants, particularly toxics. Our alternative budget would
increase all R&D to $383 million (up $176.6 million from the
Reagan budget request), broken down as follows: Air, $109.1
million; Hazardous Wastes, $100.0 million; Water, $97.3 million; Pesticides, $11.0 million; Toxics, $86.2 million.

State grants must rise substantially to help states develop
adequate programs of their own, particularly in hazardous waste
control and clean-up of toxic dumps. States already shoulder

about 85 percent of the responsibility for managing environmental clean-up programs. They cannot accept even more responsibility without additional funds. Our alternative budget of $456.7 million (up $274.7 million from the Administration request) is broken down as follows: Air, $173.4 million; Water, $143.0 million; Hazardous Wastes, $87.1 million; Toxics, $40.1 million; Pesticides $13.1 million.

The third area where the Reagan budget cripples EPA's ongoing efforts is in abatement, control, and compliance (enforcement). All of EPA's programs have suffered substantial decreases in these activities, even though new responsibilities lie ahead in all programs to control toxics and to make sure installed control equipment continues to work ("continous compliance"). In addition, the Administrator of EPA, Ms. Gorsuch, abolished the enforcement arm of EPA, crippling the agency's ability to investigate and initiate enforcement actions. Our alternative budget proposes the resurrection of the enforcement arm of EPA and provides substantial increases to allow a program that would encourage voluntary compliance with the law. Our program-by-program recommendations include: Air, $144.36 million (up from $33.4 million requested); Water, $188.48 million (up from $83.6 million requested); Toxics, $141.5 million (up from about $40 million requested); Hazardous Wastes, $132.2 million (up from about $41 million requested); and Pesticides, $90.6 million (up from about $35 million requested).

Our budget also recommends modest increases in the smaller programs (radiation, drinking water, interdisciplinary programs) and a slight cut in the noise budget, although we do not agree with the Reagan Administration proposal to eliminate this program.

This account summarizes very briefly the results of detailed work that has gone into the development of a sound operating budget for EPA. A detailed justification of the Environmental Alternative budget for EPA is contained in Shredding the Environmental Safety Net: The Full Story Behind the EPA Budget Cuts (National Wildlife Federation: February 4, 1982).

Superfund. EPA proposes to allocate $230 million to begin cleanup of 114 high priority hazardous waste dump sites. The amount is not enough to do the job.

The Superfund legislation requires EPA to clean up at least 400 sites between 1981 and 1986. The cost of cleaning up just one such site--Love Canal--will run over $20 million. This includes digging up the wastes, hauling them away to a safe disposal site, installing a tile system to drain the area, piping the effluent to treatment, placing a protective "curtain" around the area, and capping the site to prevent additional drainage. It does not include the cost of purchasing houses in the surrounding area, relocating residents, or health costs.

In addition, the cost of simply diagnosing a site to determine if it presents a threat to ground water or human health, and of containing the site through placement of a fence or other protective net around it, is at least $750,000 per site. Finally, EPA needs more people to assist states in identifying and monitoring additional sites.

Money to clean up hazardous waste dumps is appropriated from the Superfund Trust Fund. The fund is supported partly by a tax on industries that generate hazardous wastes and jointly by a federal contribution. The Reagan Administration budget analysis indicates that, even if its $230 million request for Superfund activities is appropriated, the Superfund Trust Fund will still contain a surplus of over $350 million at the end of FY 1983. Thus, enough money is available to pay for immediately needed diagnosis, containment, cleanup, and monitoring activities. We recommend that the Superfund budget authority and outlays be raised by $100 million in FY 1983.

FY 1983 TRANSPORTATION FUNCTION

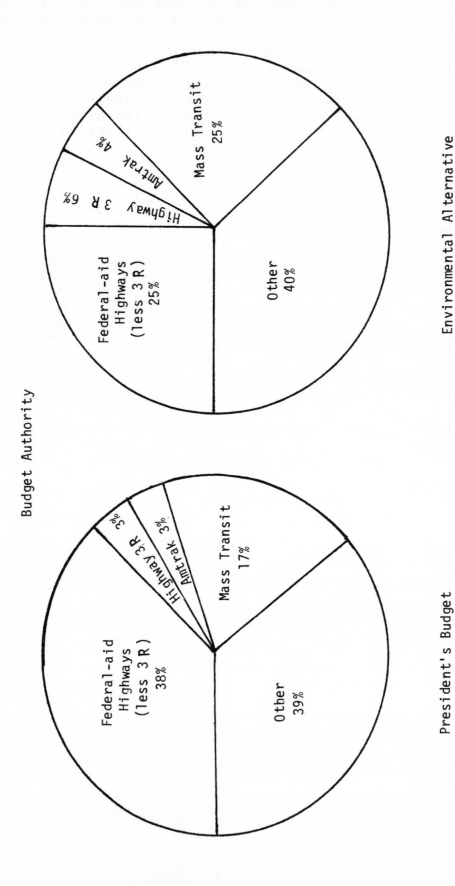

Budget Authority

Mass Transit 25%

Amtrak 4%

Highway 3 R 6%

Federal-aid Highways (less 3 R) 25%

Other 40%

Environmental Alternative

Mass Transit 17%

Highway 3 R 3%

Amtrak 3%

Federal-aid Highways (less 3 R) 38%

Other 39%

President's Budget

Introduction

The Reagan budget for transportation is misdirected. It would spend a great deal of money--$3.4 billion--for new Interstate highway construction, and far too little--$600 million--on maintenance and repair. It would continue to cut federal support for threadbare, deteriorating, but energy efficient bus and subway systems.

The Interstate highway system is 95 percent complete. The last 5 percent is inordinately expensive to build, and in most places, environmentally destructive. The Environmental Alternative budget declares the Interstate system complete. It recommends that, instead of pursuing the ever more costly and difficult goal of paving the last multi-million-dollar mile of Interstate highway, we concentrate on keeping the roads we have in good repair. It recommends a large increase over the Reagan budget in federal support for urban mass transit (up to $4.7 billion--the amount in the FY 1981 budget). We believe that support for urban public transportation is a necessary and proper federal activity since it promotes energy conservation while discouraging sprawl land use patterns. The resulting contribution to the protection of prime agricultural lands, public health, and energy independence all significantly further the security of our nation. Left unaided, states and municipalities have neither the financial ability nor the incentive to pay the upfront costs of putting efficient public transportation systems in place.

Highways
401

The Interstate System. In the past, Federal aid for highways has concentrated heavily on building the Interstate system. In FY 1981, 20 times as much federal money ($3.9 billion) went into Interstate construction as went into maintenance and repair ($200 million). The Reagan budget for FY 1983 improves the balance, but not nearly enough ($3.4 billion for construction, $600 million for repair).

The federal share to complete the remaining 5 percent of the Interstate system is estimated at $40 billion or $4 billion a year over 10 years--with no allowance for inflation. This compares with a total cost of about $76 billion for the first 95 percent.

Clearly, Interstate highway construction has entered an era of diminishing returns. Most of the unfinished segments (for example, New York's Westway--now estimated to cost $1.7 billion for a 4-mile road or about $10,000 per inch) are not only terribly costly, but are of dubious benefit, considering the environmental costs. It is for these reasons that the Environmental Alternative budget would declare the Interstate system complete. Our alternative budget for FY 1983 includes $1 billion for Interstate construction (compared with $3.4 billion for the Reagan budget) but this is only to complete unfinished contracts, not to start any new construction.

What is genuinely needed in the Interstate highway system is maintenance and repair (3R). In a February 1982 report, the Department of Transportation said that it would take spending of $1.7 billion per year to keep the Interstate system in good repair. Not only is the Reagan budget proposal of $600 million inadequate; it also expands the definition of maintenance to encompass reconstruction, which includes the construction of new lanes and interchanges. We call these activities construction and believe they should be justified as such. Our Alternative Budget proposes $1.2 billion, a doubling of the amount recommended by the Department of Transportation for maintenance and repair, to be used for these purposes only.

Other Federal-Aid Highways and Bridges. The Reagan Administration has proposed turning back to the states responsibility for maintaining roads that are not of federal significance. We agree, with the proviso that adequate federal funds for this purpose are also returned to the states. Our alternative budget provides $1.5 billion in federal funds to the states for maintenance only--not construction--of primary highways and rural and small urban roads.

There is a strong continuing federal interest in the nation's urban highway system because of the national interest in the economic vitality of our cities. The Environmental Alternative budget proposes federal spending of $700 million for the urban highway system, including the option, as present law allows, to transfer these funds to the purchase of buses or for transportation systems management.

Forty percent of the nation's 560,000 public bridges are deficient. According to a 1981 estimate, to repair or replace these bridges would cost $41 billion. Our budget includes bridge maintenance and repair as an obvious public priority, particularly when compared with new Interstate highway construction. We recommend a $900 million program for FY 83.

FEDERAL-AID HIGHWAY PROGRAM (Total Direct Program Costs)

	1981	1982	1983	ENV. ALT.
Interstate Construction	3,913	3,500	3,400	1,000
Interstate 3R	198	650	600	1,200
Primary	1,561	1,500	1,500	1,200
Rural/Small Urban	443	350	300	300
Urban System	808	500	450	700
Bridge Program	709	900	850	900
Other	1,218	800	700	700
TOTAL	8,850	8,200	7,800	6,000

Highway Safety. More than half of new cars sold today are small cars. The use of small, fuel-efficient cars is in the national interest. Thus, a strong federal commitment to small-car safety is appropriate, indeed essential. Our budget calls for continued federal support for highway safety programs, including continued state enforcement of the 55 mile per hour speed limit.

Amtrak
402

The Reagan budget cuts Amtrak funds sharply--down 18 percent in budget authority from FY 1982 to $600 million and down 26 percent in outlays, to $610 million. The Administration proposal will shrink routes, leaving more sections of the country without passenger train service and making the entire system less viable economically. The Environmental Alternative budget provides continued federal support for an effective passenger train system as an important energy-efficient alternative to the private auto.

Passenger surveys have shown that 63 percent of Amtrak passengers were traveling alone. Forty-five percent of respondents said that, without Amtrak, they would travel by car; 28 percent, by plane; 21 percent, by bus (the only alternative more energy-efficient than Amtrak); and 7 percent would forego the trip. Amtrak, the surveys indicate, can be more successful than intercity buses in attracting people to energy-efficient transportation.

Our alternative budget recommends funding of $788 million for Amtrak in FY 1983, which is the level already authorized by Congress. At this level of support, the Amtrak system will be able to make improvements, such as new equipment, improved track, and running trains of optimum size, that will enhance energy efficiency. In fact, with further improvements of this kind, and the additional passengers they should attract, the possibilities are good for a near-doubling of energy-efficiency in the Amtrak system.

Urban Mass Transportation
403

The Reagan Administration is phasing down aid to cities for capital investments in bus and subway systems, and is rapidly phasing out operating subsidies, to be totally eliminated by 1985. Proposed spending is down 10 percent from the FY 1982 levels, and 32 percent from the FY 1981 level. We believe this is a serious mistake. The United States depends on foreign nations for one-third of our oil supply. A strong mass transit system provides a good alternative to the private auto, cuts the national losses if oil prices abruptly rise or if shortages occur, and can bring about more energy-efficient patterns of city living, if combined with effective land use planning. Thus, strong mass transit contributes to our economic and national security.

Urban transit systems across the nation are in trouble. Last year, the Boston transit system shut down temporarily until it received an emergency bail-out from the state. The New York City transit system needs $1 billion per year in capital investments, but is getting only $300 million. Of the 60,000 city buses in service all over the country, 14,000 are more than 13 years old. The American Public Transit Association estimates the capital needs for bus and rail urban transit systems at $50 billion over the next 10 years.

If the federal government withdraws support for operating expenses, as the Reagan Administration plans to do, the vicious circle of higher fares, worse service, and ridership losses will continue.

The Environmental Alternative budget recommends large, reliable federal subsidies for mass transit for both capital and operating expenses. We would return federal support of mass urban transit to the level of the FY 1981 budget--$4.7 billion a year.

OTHER ENVIRONMENTAL PROGRAMS

Introduction

Much of the Environmental Alternative budget deals in billions or hundreds of millions of dollars. But some environmental programs that are of vital importance involve much smaller sums. For these programs, the difference of $1 million or $2 million, or even less, can mean life or death. Our budget analysis covers two such "small" programs--the United Nations Environment Programme and the Council on Environmental Quality.

United Nations Environment Programme
151

The internationally accepted Global 2000 study graphically portrays the massive deforestation, spread of deserts, pesticide misuse, and pollution from chemical waste which threaten the world environment. The United Nations Environment Programme was created to address these problems.

Since UNEP was established in 1972, the United States has been its key financial supporter, providing $10 million or 30 percent of the UNEP budget in fiscal years 1973 to 1981. Last year, the U.S. contribution was $7.85 million. The Reagan budget for FY 1983 would reduce the contribution to $3 million--a 61 percent drop from FY 1982.

The figure proposed by the Administration would greatly affect UNEP's ability to continue its activities, including its data collection and information systems: the Global Environment Monitoring System, the International Register of Potentially Toxic Chemicals, and the International Referral System. UNEP's ability to spark new projects in such fields as world climate, tropical deforestation, and control of desertification, would also be undercut.

Congress has already authorized FY 1982 spending for UNEP at the level of $10 million or 4.4 percent of the total appropriated for International Organizations and Conferences, whichever is lower. Thus Congress tried to assure that the small, but vital UNEP program would not be squeezed out by larger ones.

The Environmental Alternative budget recommends a UNEP appropriation of $7.6 million for FY 1983, consistent with the expressed intention of Congress. This year, many member nations are increasing their contributions to UNEP. A drastic drop in the U.S. contribution might well be seen as a withdrawal by the United States of interest in the global environment.

An important issue during the discussion of UNEP appropriations in FY 1982, and certain to be a major consideration again this year, is a Congressional study of UNEP now being conducted by the House Appropriations Sub-Committee on Foreign Operations. In any evaluation of UNEP's strengths and weaknesses, it is important to take into account the fact that UNEP is a relatively young organization and has a large mandate. We believe that continued financial support of this unique environmental program, rather than a weakened commitment to its goals, will help to ensure improvement in UNEP's effectiveness.

Council on Environmental Quality
802

The Council's ability to influence environmentally related policy decisions in the Reagan Administration is limited at best, no matter what the funding level. With the severe budget reduction in FY 1982 of $2,426,000 and a reduction from about 30 to half a dozen professional staff, the Council's traditional role in policy review and development in the Executive Office of the President has been virtually abolished. It is important, however, to give CEQ enough funding for oversight of regulations related to environmental impact analysis, as required by the National Environmental Policy Act, and to participate in the resolution of NEPA-related disputes in the Executive branch. The Reagan budget proposes a funding level of $926,000 for CEQ. Our Alternative budget proposes an increase of 25 percent, which should be enough to allow the Council to oversee NEPA regulations.

Our proposal for a minimal increase in CEQ's funding should not be interpeted as approval of what has happened to CEQ under the Reagan Administration. Rather, it is a recognition that the President relies on the Secretary of the Interior and the Administrator of EPA for leadership in developing environmental policy and that CEQ has been relegated to a minor role.

ALTERNATIVE BUDGET PROPOSALS
For the Environment
($ in millions)

	Agency	1981 ACTUAL BA	1981 ACTUAL O	1982 ESTIMATE BA	1982 ESTIMATE O
270	ENERGY				
271	SOLAR ENERGY & RENEWABLE R & D	471.0	561.0	265.0	496.0
271	(DOE) NUCLEAR PROGRAMS	1,049.0	1,124.0	1,087.0	1,184.0
271	SYNTHETIC FUELS CORP.	35.0	6.2	41.6	24.5
272	(DOE) ENERGY CONSERVATION	675.9	708.0	386.1	740.0
272	(HUD) SOLAR & ENERGY CONSERVATION BANK	--	--	23.0	6.5
300	NATURAL RESOURCES AND ENVIRONMENT				
301	WATER RESOURCES DEVELOPMENT	4,165.6	4,217.5	3,916.1	4,093.4
302	U.S. FOREST SERVICE OPS.	2,283.0	2,154.0	1,951.0	2,137.0
302	BUREAU OF LAND MGT. OPS.	1,035.4	1,031.8	1,139.1	1,118.2
302	OFFICE OF SURFACE MINING	177.9	131.1	160.5	136.9
302	COASTAL ZONE MANAGEMENT	51.6	54.9	7.4	44.6
303	LAND AND WATER CONSERVATION FUND	288.6	495.0	149.2	484.9
303	FISH AND WILDLIFE SERVICE OPERATIONS*	424.2	463.1	418.1	408.5
303	NATIONAL PARK SERVICE OPS.	552.9	606.2	647.2	660.2
303	HISTORIC PRESERVATION FUND	26.0	52.6	25.4	44.3
303	URBAN PARKS RECOVERY PROGRAM	1.0	18.4	7.7	64.4
303	YOUTH CONSERVATION EMPLOYMENT (ENC. YACC)	168.0	176.0	62.26	62.6
304	ENVIRONMENTAL PROTECTION AGENCY				
	Salaries and Expenses	561.7	543.4	555.1	597.5
	Buildings and Facilities	4.1	1.5	3.6	3.5
	Research and Development	250.5	247.0	154.4	206.5
	Abatement, Control and Compliance	534.8	559.4	372.9	453.4
	TOTAL EPA OPPERATING BUDGET	1,351.1	1,351.3	1,086.0	1,261.0
304	SUPERFUND	74.7	8.0	190.0	117.7

*Exclusive of wetland loan advance

	Agency	1981 ACTUAL BA	1981 ACTUAL O	1982 ESTIMATE BA	1982 ESTIMATE O
400	TRANSPORTATION				
401	FEDERAL-AID HIGHWAYS	9,045.0	8,821.6	8,271.4	8,024.0
401	NATIONAL HIGHWAY TRAFFIC SAFETY ADMINISTRATION	191.4	278.1	177.4	262.4
402	AMTRAK	881.0	851.0	735.0	820.0
403	URBAN MASS TRANS.	4,727.0	3,917.0	3,546.0	3,817.0
	MISC. PROGRAMS				
802	COUNCIL ON ENVIRONMENTAL QUALITY	2.5	2.6	.9	1.2
151	U.N. ENVIRONMENTAL PROGRAMME	10.0	10.0	10.0	7.8

REAGAN 1983		ENV. ALT. 1983		CHANGE FR ADM.			
BA	O	BA	O	BA		O	
73.0	159.2	275.0	236.0	+	202.0	+	76.8
1,016.0	980.0	723.0	769.0	−	293.0	−	211.0
44.9	35.5	0	0	−	44.9	−	35.5
21.8	335.6	575.1	600.0	+	553.3	+	264.4
0	15.0	100.0	45.0	+	100.0	+	30.0
3,825.0	3,857.0	3,225.0	3,257.0	−	600.0	−	600.0
2,132.0	2,173.0	2,032.0	2,073.0	−	100.0	−	100.0
1,255.6	1,229.4	1,260.1	1,249.6	+	4.5	+	20.2
159.8	146.3	160.5	156.3	+	0.7	+	10.0
6.4	27.7	48.0	37.0	+	41.6	+	9.3
69.4	271.3	400.0	496.3	+	330.6	+	225.0
412.4	383.1	432.5	389.6	+	20.1	+	6.5
674.8	672.6	674.8	672.6		0		0
0	22.8	30.0	32.8	+	30.0	+	10.0
0	38.6	20.0	48.6	+	20.0	+	10.0
0	0	250.0	200.0	+	250.0	+	200.0
538.1	548.9	1,162.0	1,161.4				
3.0	3.6	3.0	3.6				
108.7	165.6	254.1	254.1				
311.6	387.2	759.4	759.4				
961.4	1,105.0	2,178.5	2,178.5	+1,217.2		+1,073.5	
230.0	188.0	330.0	288.0	+	100.0	+	100.0
7,800.0	8,026.0	6,000.0	6,625.0	− 1,800.0		− 1,401.0	
183.1	184.3	184.4	237.0	+	1.3	+	52.7
600.0	610.0	788.0	798.0	+	188.0	+	188.0
3,202.0	3,221.0	4,700.0	3,900.0	+1,498.0		+	679.9
.9	1.2	1.2	1.2	+	.3		0
10.0	3.0	10.0	7.6		0	+	4.6

NET CHANGE IN EXPENDITURES: +1,719.7   + 603.4

121

REVENUES

ROYALTIES AND USER FEES

Introduction

The commercially valuable resources on and under public lands belong to all U.S. citizens. When private individuals mine gold on federally owned lands, or drill for oil and gas, or cut timber, or graze cattle, they should pay the owners full value for the use of these resources, equal to what a private landowner would receive.

Similarly, when the government provides special services to individuals for commercial purposes, those individuals should pay for it. Some government activities, such as cleaning up the nation's air and water, benefit all citizens, and all of us rightly pay for them through taxes. Other activities, such as building highways for truck use, providing irrigation water to farmers, or dredging ports and channels for vessel traffic, are clearly beneficial to special users on a dollars and cents basis. If the general taxpayer, rather than the commercial user, pays for these services, then the government is subsidizing the users.

Economic justice is not the only issue involved in the full collection of royalties and the imposition of user fees. Subsidies affect economic efficiency as well. A businessman who pays all the costs of an enterprise will be more careful in his investment than one who is getting a hidden subsidy.

Protection of natural resources is also at stake. For example, when grazing fees per animal on public lands are a fraction of the fees on privately owned lands, this subsidy encourages overgrazing and the ruination of the land. Government-subsidized timber sales encourage overcutting of our national forests, and discourage investment in privately owned forestland.

The Reagan Administration has declared its opposition to subsidies, and its support of user fees and full collection of royalties. The Administration has taken steps to reform the management of oil and gas royalties for federal lands. It supports user fees for ports and waterways and a waste management fee for nuclear reactor operators. We applaud these moves by the Reagan Administration, but we also believe they can be taken much further.

For the public lands, the Reagan Administration has made no proposals for a user fee system. Instead, it proposes to sell off federal property, including National Forest and Bureau of Land Management lands, to the "Sagebrush Rebels." The Reagan budget projects a FY 1983 revenue of $1 billion for the sale of federal properties, including public lands.

The Administration proposes to sell as much as 35 million acres over a five year period. This sale is most ill advised. Although some surplus government properties are clearly suitable for sale, it is not in the national interest to sell for one-time profit lands which generate continuing revenues from mineral, timber, and grazing activities. Given the potential for user-fee and royalty revenues from the lands currently held in public ownership, such sales cannot be considered a wise use of valuable resources. Land sales would also, of course, preclude multiple use management and adequate environmental protection for important national lands and resources.

In the following section, our Environmental Alternative budget proposes a number of ideas for equitable, economically sound collection of fees and royalties which will also have the effect of conserving natural resources and protecting the natural environment. Our list is not comprehensive. Even so, we calculate that the government could collect an additional $4.5 billion a year, from the additional royalty collections and user fees we propose.

Improved Oil and Gas Royalty Recovery
271

Every year, the federal government loses hundreds of millions of dollars due to the mismanagement of royalty collections. The General Accounting Office and the Commission on Fiscal Accountability of the Nation's Energy Resources have indicated that 7 to 10 percent of all royalties due the federal government are lost due to mismanagement. In addition, as much as 2 to 6 percent of royalties for oil may be lost due to oil theft.

The Secretary of the Interior has said he will take immediate action to end mismanagement and theft in royalty collection. The federal budget for FY 1983 should reflect these recovered funds. Improved royalty management should bring into the U.S. Treasury an additional 270 to 387 million dollars in FY 1983 (not including Indian and State revenues). Effective measures to prevent theft could raise further the amount of royalties collected.

The Environmental Alternative budget includes $300 million in revenue gains from better management of oil and gas royalties.

Additional Royalties for Onshore Oil and Gas
271

The federal government continues to charge different royalty rates for onshore and offshore oil and gas leases. The Commission on Fiscal Accountability recently recommended that the federal royalty rate be increased from 12-1/2 percent to a minimum of 16-2/3 percent for onshore oil and gas leases. In its explanation, the Commission noted that there appeared to be no reason for the disparity. Furthermore, increases in royalty rates received by private landholders have been increasing.

While oil prices have soared and private landowners have been negotiating royalty rates of 33-1/3 percent and above for land leased to oil and gas companies the Interior Department has shown little initiative in raising royalty rates on federal lands. In fact, the Department proposed to reduce offshore royalty rates for FY 1983, to equalize them with onshore rates.

The Department's authority to raise royalty rates for onshore leases is limited, since the rate is established by law for noncompetitive leases. The Department can, however, request that Congress change the law, and can make a persuasive case for doing so.

We agree with the Commission's recommendation to increase royalty rates to a minimum of 16-2/3 percent, provided that the increase is properly treated as a minimum. The Congress should consider giving DOI the authority to revise royalty rates for onshore leases, as it does for offshore leases (but not below the minimum). Then DOI should annually review private royalty agreements to insure that the Federal Treasury is receiving a fair return. The continuing treatment of federal lands as bargain-basement discounts for oil and gas developers contributes to the pressure for increased leasing of federal lands in environmentally sensitive areas.

The added revenue from raising royalty rates for onshore leases would be minimal for FY 1983--$1 to $3 million even if Congress and DOI act promptly. But by 1990, increased royalties could total at least $100 million annually. If the value of oil and gas increases, the royalties will increase correspondingly, with a still greater return to the federal Treasury.

Additional revenues could also be raised by auctioning on-shore leases, as is done for offshore leases, rather than the current system of drawing names in a lottery. Innovative variations in leases, bonuses, royalties, and profit-sharing have been devised which can increase government revenues from both offshore and onshore lands.

Fair Market Pricing of Uranium Enrichment Services
271

The federal government operates three plants that enrich uranium for use in nuclear reactors. The government provides this service for all domestic and some foreign utilities, with prices set to recover direct government costs. Adoption of "fair market pricing," comparable to what a private business would charge, would eliminate a subsidy to the nuclear industry that the Department of Energy has estimated to total $5.5 billion during the 1954-1980 period (1979 dollars). This reform was advocated by Presidents Ford and Carter, and was actually enacted by Congress in 1977 in a bill that was vetoed over a different issue. The General Accounting Office has repeatedly examined the issue and strongly recommended this policy revision.

Fair market pricing would promote efficiency and equity in the production of uranium fuel and the generation of electric power. It is time to place this government activity on a more businesslike basis, and send the appropriate signal to the marketplace about the relative values of conservation and consumption of enriched uranium. The latest estimate by the Congressional Budget Office shows federal revenues to increase by $525 million in FY 1983 resulting from fair market pricing. Our budget adopts this estimate.

User Fees for Ports and Waterways
301

The federal government will spend about $7.5 billion for building and maintaining inland waterways during the next five years. Of this, only about $440 million will be recovered through the existing tax on commercial barge fuel. Thus, the

125

federal government will be subsidizing the commercial craft that use these waterways in the amount of $7 billion over the 1982-1986 period. In addition, the Army Corps of Engineers spends over $500 million a year on improving and maintaining deep draft ports and harbors, to accommodate oceangoing vessels. Outlays over the next five years are estimated at $3.3 billion. Much of this subsidy goes to foreign-owned vessels.

Much of the harbor dredging and canal digging that keeps these ports and waterways navigable has harmful environmental effects on rivers, bays, and wetlands. Often these activities seriously reduce populations of sport fish, commercial fish, and wildlife. User fees promote efficiency in transportation investments, which translates into less demand on natural resources.

President Reagan has recommended legislation to increase user fees for deepdraft harbors and inland waterways, to yield an estimated $519 million in FY 83. We strongly support the Administration proposal.

Grazing Fees
302

Charging market value for livestock grazing leases on federal lands would bring in substantial additional revenues and would also help to protect the badly overgrazed public lands from further damage.

Grazing fees on lands managed by the Forest Service and the Bureau of Land Management are determined by a formula which Congress established in 1978. The formula includes an index for "ability to pay," which is affected by beef cattle prices and cost of production. Application of the formula has resulted in a 38 percent reduction of publc land grazing fees in the past year, while the average lease rate for private grazing land rose 12 percent. In 1982, the public land grazing fee, set according to the formula, will be $1.86 per animal unit month (AUM), which is the grazing of one cow, one horse, or five sheep in one month. This compares with a private grazing lease rate of $8.83 per AUM. The artifically cheap price for grazing on the public lands positively invites overgrazing.

In FY 1983, under the present system, the Forest Service and BLM will collect $30.1 million in grazing fees. Fifty percent of this goes to the land management agencies for range improvements, 25 percent goes to the county in which the grazing land is located and 25 percent goes to the U.S. Treasury.

Our alternative budget recommends that grazing fees on public lands be set roughly equal to those received by the Defense Department, which leases grazing lands in New Mexico under a competitive bidding system. With this reform, the U.S. Treasury should collect an additional $99 million in grazing fees in FY 1983 (including the amounts returned to the counties and those used for range management).

Ocean Dumping Fee
304

The ocean has traditionally been a cost-free and convenient place to dump many materials which are hard to dispose of on land. Control over the ocean dumping of harmful materials was established by law ten years ago, with deadlines set to phase out the dumping of harmful sewage sludge. During 1980, 110 million tons of material--sewage sludge, industrial waste, and dredge spoil--were dumped into the ocean under regulations and permits issued by the Corps of Engineers and the Environmental Protection Agency. The deadlines for stopping the dumping of harmful sewage sludge have been repeatedly postponed, and pressure is mounting to loosen standards and allow increased volumes of dumping in future years.

The Environmental Alternative budget proposes a fee of two dollars per ton on all materials dumped into the ocean. Such fees would be charged to the holders of EPA dumping permits or, in the case of dredge spoil from a navigation project, the non-federal project sponsor. The dumping fee would supplement regulatory control, deter unnecessary ocean dumping, and spur the search for economical, environmentally sound alternatives. It should recover at least a part of the environmental and administrative costs associated with ocean dumping.

Our alternative budget includes $250 million in additional revenues from the ocean dumping fee.

For the hardrock minerals--gold, silver, uranium, copper, lead, cobalt and many others--there is at present no royalty at all for production from federally-owned land. Under the 1872 Mining Law, which still governs hardrock minerals, a miner can stake a claim and hold it for no more than the cost of annual "assessment work"--a pro forma requirement for $100 of work a year. When miners produce minerals from the claims, the proceeds are all theirs. The government receives nothing. Moreover, a miner can "patent" his claim, thus gaining ownership of the land as well as the minerals under it, for $2.50 to $5.00 an acre--the same price he would have paid in 1872.

Such fees hardly provide an equitable return to the landowners (i.e., U.S. citizens) from an industry in which domestic raw material production was valued at $25 billion for 1981. The federal government does not presently keep track of the value of hardrock mineral production from public lands. The Office of Technology Assessment has conservatively estimated the annual value of nonfuel hardrock minerals production from the public lands at $12 to $15 billion per year.

We support the establishment of a minimum royalty of 16-2/3 percent for public lands minerals production, which would be commensurate with the existing base royalty levied on oil and gas production from offshore leases. Such a royalty would result in at least $2 billion in new revenues annually and would provide a reasonable return on the exploitation of public resources.

Heavy Truck Highway User Fees
401

The Highway Trust Fund clearly states that users should pay equitably into the fund, in proportion to the benefits they receive. This is not the case today. Numerous studies have shown that heavy trucks are not paying enough taxes to cover the costs of damage they do to roads. The Environmental Alternative budget proposes an increase of $1.3 billion in heavy truck user fees in 1983.

The deterioration of the nation's highways stems from many factors, including weather, the natural aging process, and failure to spend enough on maintenance. However, the increasing number and weight of heavy trucks on the roads is accelerating the deterioration. While autos have decreased from 82 percent to 69 percent of the traffic stream in the last 10 years, heavy trucks have increased from 7 percent to 10 percent. In 1975, the federal truck weight limits were raised from 73,280 to 80,000 pounds. Most of our highways, including Interstates, were designed to carry the lower weight. Increased axle weights have an exponential effect in the damage they do. One 5-axle truck loaded to the 80,000-pound federal limit does as much damage as 9,600 autos weighing a total of 28 million pounds.

A 1978 Georgia study found that 4-axle and 5-axle trucks paid only 51 percent of their cost responsibility in highway fees. Oregon, Florida, and other states have made similar findings. A recent study by the federal Department of Transportation found that heavy trucks covered only 63 percent of their cost responsibility for damage to federally funded highways in 1977. They paid $1.2 billion in taxes while their true responsibility was $1.9 billion, a shortfall of $700 million. The study projected that the underpayment will be nearly $1.6 billion by 1985, if the present tax structure continues.

The Reagan budget proposes no increase in user fees for heavy trucks. Our alternative budget calls for an increase of $1.3 billion in heavy truck user fees in 1983 to correct the inequities of the present tax structure.

Federal Parking Fees
802

Even in these times of budget austerity, the federal government has continued to provide free parking to employees at government facilities around the country. We propose to save energy, space, and money by means of a fee for federal parking at rates comparable to those charged by the private sector. In those suburban and rural areas where private parking is customarily free of charge, no fee would be charged.

The subsidy involved in free federal parking will continue to bias drivers' decisions toward the use of private automobiles and away from more energy efficient means of transportation. This inducement to drive is particularly inappropriate in the Washington, D.C. area, the largest concentration of Federal employment in the nation. The region is the beneficiary of a major federal investment in a 100-mile subway system, designed in large part to serve federal employment centers. (Capitol Hill, with its 10,000 free parking spaces, is now served by two subway stations close to Congressional office buildings.) Continued free federal parking jeopardizes the financial stability of this multi-billion-dollar investment, and further delays the achievement of regional air quality standards. Similar effects are to be found in other cities with large numbers of federal employees.

For FY 1983, the Environmental Alternative budget recommends the establishment of parking fees at federal facilities at prevailing commercial rates, yielding $30 million to the Treasury.

TAX EXPENDITURES

Introduction

Tax expenditures are losses in revenues arising from special selective exemptions for certain groups of taxpayers, sets of economic activities, or sectors of the economy. They are a hidden form of subsidy. They are meant to encourage a desired activity, or help a certain kind of taxpayer. In this way, tax expenditures resemble many government spending or loan programs.

But while the goals of tax expenditures and direct spending may be alike, the approach and results are quite different. Direct spending programs are reviewed each year by Congress as part of the budget process. They are compared explicitly against each other and shaped by the overall budget ceiling. Tax expenditures, by contrast, tend to take on a life of their own. They are not regularly scrutinized by Congress. How much they will actually cost the Treasury is not certain, and may be confirmed only after all the taxpayers' returns are in. They add up to a very large hidden budget--$266 billion in 1982, or one-third as much as the direct spending which is on display in the regular budget.

We consider tax expenditures in the energy, natural resource, and environment area far too important a subject to be ignored. Special tax exemptions can serve worthy purposes. On the other hand, they can long outlive their usefulness without ever attracting much attention. They may enrich some taxpayers unfairly at the expense of others. They can distort economic forces, misdirecting investment and causing wasteful, harmful consumption of natural resources.

The Environmental Alternative budget examines several natural resource, environment, and energy-related tax loopholes of dubious worth, and proposes their repeal. Their collective cost to the Treasury would be $4.4 billion in FY 1983. We also recommend the extension of a program of tax credits for energy conservation by industry, due to expire at the end of 1982.

We have by no means examined the whole gamut of energy and natural resource-related tax expenditures. In general, we favor the continuation of a whole group of tax credits, for businesses and homeowners, that will encourage the use of struggling new technologies for energy conservation, solar energy, and other renewable energy sources. Altogether, these tax credits will cost the Treasury less than $1 billion in

FY 1983. All of them have defined expiration dates, which means that the Congress must reexamine them rather than letting them linger indefinitely without attention.

The older, far larger tax expenditures favoring producers of oil and gas, coal, and other minerals have no such sunset provisions. It is high time to reexamine them.

Expensing of Intangible Oil and Gas Drilling Costs
271

A provision of the Internal Revenue Code dating back to 1917 allows oil and gas companies to take an immediate write-off for labor, supply, and testing costs incurred in exploring for and developing oil and gas reserves. This "expensing of intangibles" amounts to a 100 percent depreciation of investment in the first year. Businesses in general are required to spread deductible costs over the life of the capital investment. This special provision for the oil companies means they receive all the tax benefits at once, so that the first year's taxes are, in effect, deferred to a later year. This deferred tax amounts to an interest-free loan from the rest of America's taxpayers.

At one time, free interest may not have appeared too great a cost for the public to pay for encouraging new energy development. Today, high oil prices provide powerful incentives for energy exploration. On a large scale the costs of expensing of intangibles become quite significant. They translate into benefits of several billion dollars a year to companies which reaped 42 percent of the net income of the Fortune 500 in 1980. This subsidy is uneconomic and may encourage wasteful production and consumption of oil, rather than conservation.

The expensing of intangibles is the reason that many independent oil companies (which are only in the business of crude oil production) pay no taxes at all. The Citizens for Tax Justice reported a random survey of 25 independent oil companies which showed that while their 1974 average rate of return on investment was a very profitable 26 percent, most paid no income taxes. These companies receive a full write-off for the holes that prove dry. But the expensing of intangibles gives the companies almost the same tax break--about 75 percent of the total investment--for producing wells.

The Environmental Alternative budget proposes to eliminate oil industry tax deductions for expensing of intangibles. The result should be increased revenues of $3.5 billion for FY 1983.

Capital Gains Treatment of Royalties on Coal
271

In the Revenue Act of 1951, Congress provided that royalties on coal could be treated as capital gains rather than income, and taxed at the lower capital gains rates. The provision was intended to encourage leasing and production of coal. Today, coal bearing lands under lease exceed potential demand for at least a decade. The provision has outlived its original purpose, and stands to become a growing windfall as the value of coal increases. Use of this antiquated provision may be more profitable to taxpayers than the depletion allowance.

The Environmental Alternative budget proposes to eliminate capital gains treatment of coal royalties, for a revenue gain of $120 million for FY 1983.

Industrial Energy Conservation Tax Credit
272

The existing 10 percent tax credit for industrial energy conservation investments expires at the end of 1982. Most of the credits have been used to pay for equipment that cuts energy consumption by capturing and using waste heat.

We believe that this tax credit is well worth extending. It can make important contributions to conservation in existing industrial plants, half of which will probably still be in use at the end of the century. It not only heightens management's awareness of conservation, but much more importantly, improves corporate cash flow for conservation investments. Low cash flow is one major reason why cost-effective industrial energy conservation opportunities are being neglected.

Our alternative budget recommends extension of this tax credit through the end of 1985, when several tax credits for business investment in solar and renewable energy are due to expire. The cost in revenues for FY 1983 is estimated at $500 million. The Reagan budget provides $320 million in FY 1983 for continuing or deferred expenditures under this program.

Capital Gains Treatment of Timber
302

Income from harvested timber held at least one year before cutting is now given preferential capital gains rates. This tax subsidy is unnecessary and inappropriate. It is especially inappropriate for timber harvests from federal lands, where other subsidies are available to producers. Timber producers can also take advantage of several other favorable tax provisions. The capital gains tax provision, triggered by the timber harvest, distorts the structure of the industry and its investment decisions. Usually, natural resources are allocated most efficiently when extractive industries are required to internalize their costs of production. Signals provided by the marketplace against overharvest, (i.e., lower prices) ought not be blurred by overly generous tax treatment of income from timber harvesting.

The latest estimate by the Congressional Budget Office shows federal revenues would increase by $300 million in FY 1983 if this provision were eliminated. Our budget incorporates this estimate.

Tax Exemptions for Nonfuel Minerals
306

The depletion allowance for nonfuel minerals will be worth $435 million to the industry in FY 1983 and will cause a corresponding loss of revenues to the U.S. Treasury. Expensing of mining exploration costs will result in the loss of another $30 million in tax revenues for FY 1983.

In 1975, Congress mandated a phaseout of the 22 percent depletion allowance for oil and gas; the allowance is now available only to smaller independent crude oil producers, and is being reduced to 15 percent by 1984. Most nonfuel mineral producers still qualify for the 22 percent depletion--ironically, in view of the rapidly expanding participation by the oil industry in the nonfuel minerals business.

In effect, the nonfuels mineral industry already receives a hefty subsidy from the federal government because no royalties are paid for production of these minerals from federal lands. Tax exemptions of $465 million add another hidden subsidy. One effect of such subsidies is to encourage consumption, discouraging conservation alternatives such as recycling and reuse.

The Environmental Alternative budget recommends that the depletion allowance and expensing deductions for nonfuel mineral production be eliminated, thus producing additional revenues of $465 million for FY 1983.

Personal Tax Deductions for Interest on Second and Third Homes
371

Home mortgage interest payments have always been deductible under the federal income tax, mainly to promote home ownership, civic involvement and better home maintenance. Providing federal tax subsidies to second and third homes does not promote these goals. Rather, it serves as a financial incentive for speculative development--often expensive subdivisions in ecologically sensitive areas such as seashores and mountains. At a time when the nation is falling far short of meeting its primary housing needs, this deduction raises serious equity questions as well. Eliminating the federal tax subsidy for this type of personal expenditure will not eliminate second and third home construction. It will, however, raise some $400 million in additional revenue in FY 1983, and in future years should reduce the attractiveness of large scale vacation home development.

REVENUES AND OFFSETTING RECEIPTS
(in millions of dollars)

Royalties and User Fees

271	Fair Market Pricing of Uranium Enrichment Services	+	525
271	Improved Oil & Gas Royalty Collection	+	300
302	Grazing Fees	+	100
304	Ocean Dumping Fee	+	250
306	Royalties for Hard Rock Minerals	+	2,000
401	Heavy Truck Highway User Fees	+	1,300
802	Federal Parking Fees	+	30
	Subtotal – Royalties and User Fees	+	4,505

Tax Expenditures

271	Expensing of Intangible Oil & Gas Drilling Costs	+	3,500
271	Capital Gains Treatment of Royalties on Coal	+	120
272	Industry Energy Conservation Credit	–	180
302	Capital Gains Treatment of Timber	+	300
306	Tax Exemptions for Nonfuel Minerals	+	465
371	Personal Tax Deductions for Interest on 2nd and 3rd Homes	+	400
	Subtotal – Tax Expenditures	+	4,605

Total – Revenues and Offsetting Receipts   + 9,110

SPONSORING ORGANIZATIONS

The Environmental Alternative Budget provides an overview of our budget proposals. For further details and background on these recommendations the following organizations should be contacted:

Environmental Policy Center
Contact: Brent Blackwelder (202) 547-5330

Friends of the Earth
Contact: Liz Kaplan (202) 543-4312

Izaak Walton League of America
Contact: Maitland Sharpe (301) 528-1818

National Audubon Society
Contact: Alison Horton (202) 547-9009

National Parks and Conservation Association
Contact: William Lienesch (202) 265-2717

National Wildlife Federation
Contact: Edward Osann (202) 797-6865

Natural Resources Defense Council
Contact: Jonathan Lash (202) 223-8210

Preservation Action
Contact: Nellie Longworth (202) 659-0915

Sierra Club
Contact: Larry Williams (202) 547-1141

Solar Lobby
Contact: Sam Enfield (202) 466-6350

The Wilderness Society
Contact: Ronald Tipton (202) 828-6600

Citizen's Guide to Action

WHAT TO DO IF YOU'RE OUTRAGED

No one can possibly do all the things suggested below. Pick one or two that appeal to you, or think up even better ideas. Let us know what works best.

Media

- Review the book for your local paper or your organization's newsletter.

- Call talk shows, mention the book, and offer to appear live to discuss the Reagan environmental program. If you can't get into the studio, call in and discuss the book with the host over the telephone. Emphasize the local effects.

- Gather a few friends to meet with the editorial boards of your local papers.

- Write letters to the editors of your local paper and your favorite news journal, citing the Reagan policies that will affect you or community most directly.

Politics

If you're a DEMOCRAT, the value of the evidence in this book
is obvious. If you're a REPUBLICAN, suggest to your local party
leaders that continued allegiance to the Reagan environmental program
is going to make for some mighty slippery coattails in upcoming
elections. Remind them that much of what Mr. Reagan is dismantling
is Republican policy, reaching back past his beloved Coolidge to
Teddy Roosevelt, even Abe Lincoln. The Democrats avoided Carter
in the 1980 elections; Republicans may want to rethink Reagan.

• Suggest that local service clubs, union locals, churches, garden
  clubs, outings groups, medical groups, student associations,
  neighborhood associations, and civic organizations sponsor debates
  based on the charges in this book. Invite local candidates to
  participate.

• Invite candidates for local offices to your home for a neighborhood
  meeting. Display the book and keep environmental subjects central
  to the discussion. Suggest that opposition to the Reagan environmental program is good politics.

• Draft a resolution criticizing the Reagan environmental program and submit it to your city council or county board of supervisors. Work with a member or employee of the council or board to get the language just right.

- Telephone the local offices of your Senators and Representative. Find out which aide works on environmental matters. Ask the aide to insert an article based on the book into the <u>Congressional Record</u>. If the answer is yes, draft such an article.

Local Organizing

- Offer to speak to local clubs, unions, service organizations, churches, and the like.

- Offer to debate the Reagan environmental program before local clubs, etc.

- Produce a flier based on the book, perhaps concentrating on the local effects of the Reagan program. Distribute the flier at supermarkets, movie theaters, or house-to-house. Use the flier to recruit people to work in upcoming election campaigns.

- Produce a display using the book and clippings from newspapers and magazines. Set it up in stores and other public places.

- Use the book as a calling card to broaden the environmental coalition. Meet with people from unions, health organizations, minority groups. Discuss the impact Reagan's environmental program will have. Find areas of agreement and decide what can be done together.

- Urge local bookstores to carry the book; they can order it from FOE.

- Carry out the "Plan of Fifteen": discuss the book with five friends, five relatives, and five people where you work.

- Promote the book by having a mailing party. Invite friends and have each one write ten postcards to their friends telling them about the book.

- Talk to Federal agency people in your area--EPA, National Park Service, U.S. Fish and Wildlife Service, National Marine Fisheries Service, etc.--and assess the local impacts of Reagan's budget cuts. Ask what programs are being cut, whether people are being fired, and what level of environmental protection the agency can now provide.

- Produce a 20-minute slide show on environmental problems in your

community: smokestacks, oily water, filled wetland areas, erosion,
landfills and other environmental problems. Write up a script
for each picture relating the problems to the Reagan administration's
lack of concern for environmental problems. Offer the slide show
to other environmental groups and school, church or other community
groups. (It is best to call up such organizations, talk with the
program director and try to schedule yourself into a regular
meeting.)

    *   *   *   *

ABOVE ALL (and easiest of all): If you agree with the charges
in this book, and the environmentalists' counter proposals,
write to your Senator and your congressional representatives,
and let them know how you feel about James Watt, Anne Gorsuch,
and, above all, Ronald Reagan and his policies toward resources,
energy, and public health.

We'd like to keep in touch with you!

Please clip and mail:

```
---------------------------------------------
|                                           |
| To: FOE, 4512 University Way, Seattle WA 98105 |
|                                           |
| Name_____   |
|                                           |
| Address_____   |
|                                           |
|        _____   |
|                                           |
| Phones (home)_____(work)_____ |
|                                           |
| I can help:                               |
|                                           |
| _____organize in my community           |
|                                           |
| _____work in political campaigns        |
|                                           |
| _____analyze local effects of the Reagan program |
|                                  (RRAE)   |
|                                           |
---------------------------------------------
```

Earth Needs More Friends

And so does Friends of the Earth. Not that the friends we've got haven't performed near-miracles. They have. They've enabled FOE to play a leading role in unmasking the "peaceful atom," in espousing a soft energy path, in strengthening the Clean Air Act, in getting (after lo, these many years) stripmine control legislation through Congress, in rallying support for endangered marine mammals, in debunking the SST, in developing and pushing proposals to save Alaskan wilderness, in opposing public works boondoggles, in exposing the undesirability (not to mention the impossibility) of incessant material growth, and in striving for the preservation, restoration, and rational use of Earth and its resources.

FOE has never been large, as membership organizations go. This has made it easier, no doubt, for us to be quick-reacting and maneuverable. But there are times when there's no substitute for sheer muscle — and organizational muscle, in the view of many politicians and publicists, is strictly proportional to membership size. More members, more muscle. (More money, too, a fact we can't afford to ignore.) So one of the most crucial ways you can help FOE defend our planetary habitat is by helping us to enroll new members. Please bring the membership coupon, below, to the attention of someone who shares our concerns. Thank you.

- -

Friends of the Earth ● 1045 Sansome, #404 ● San Francisco, Calif. 94111 ● (415) 433-7373

Please enroll me as checked, at the old rates, including **Not Man Apart** and discounts on selected FOE books.

☐ Regular, $25 a year;   ☐ Contributing, $60 a year;   ☐ Life, $1,000;   ☐ Retired, $12 a year;
☐ Supporting, $35 a year;   ☐ Sustaining, $250 a year;   ☐ Student, $12 a year; ☐ Patron, $5,000 or more
☐ Sponsor = $100   ☐ Spouse = add $5 to any membership

(Name) _____

(Address) _____

(City, State, Zip) _____

(Contributions to FOE are not **tax-deductible**.)